PARISH MINISTRY
FOR RETURNING CATHOLICS

by
Patricia Barbernitz

PAULIST PRESS
New York/Mahwah, N.J.

Library of Congress Cataloging-in-Publication Data

Barbernitz, Patricia.
    Parish ministry for returning Catholics/by Patricia Barbernitz.
        p.   cm.
    Includes bibliographical references.
    ISBN 0-8091-3441-1
    1. Church work with ex-church members—Catholic Church. 2. Catholic Church—Membership. 3. Catholic Church—Adult education. 4. Catholics—Religious life. I. Title.
BX2347.8.E82B37   1993
259'.08'822–dc20   93-5901
                                                                          CIP

Published by Paulist Press
997 Macarthur Blvd.
Mahwah, N.J. 07430

Printed and bound in the United States of America

CONTENTS

This book is dedicated:
…to Father Alvin Illig, C.S.P., whose love for the inactive knew no bounds;

and

…to St. Joseph Catholic Community, where returning Catholics find a welcome haven, and where the community grapples together with the challenge of being mature Christians in the spirit of Vatican II.

INTRODUCTION

Until fairly recently, there were only Catholics. Some were "good" Catholics—they were regular church-goers, contributing to collections, sending their children to Catholic schools, helping at bingo or chicken dinners when Father asked. Some were "not so good" Catholics—they didn't go to church, didn't send their children to Catholic schools; sometimes they did still contribute to collections and help at bingo if Father asked. They hoped for a priest at their deathbed, and their good Catholic family and friends hoped for the same.

Or so it seemed.

Then came the council....and liturgical renewal...and the pill....and religion texts called "Peace, Love, Joy"...and space travel....and parish councils and corporators. And suddenly there weren't just Catholics anymore. Now there were those who called themselves ex-Catholics—some who just gave up and left the church, some who say the church just left them. There were angry, hurt or confused Catholics who couldn't feel at home in their church anymore. There were young Catholics who simply began to say NO in ways never heard of before. There were struggling Catholics who questioned and studied and tried hard to stay part of their church. There were lay leaders who were called to roles in the church formerly held only by priests or sisters.

There were—and are—returning Catholics who have been away for a long time, and are asking for more on their return journey than just an experience of Saturday afternoon confession.

Parishes today are called to offer special help and attention to these people. We must find the programs, communities and rituals that will support our sisters and brothers who are feeling drawn back to our community of faith. In one sense we owe them special attention

1

because they are part of the family; in another sense it is often hardest to minister to them because of some underlying attitudes that are like the older brother in the story of the prodigal son: "I hung in there. Why didn't you?"

This book seeks to help parishes prepare to minister to returning Catholics. Chapter 1 reminds us who they are; Chapter 2 challenges us to invite them back; Chapters 3, 4, 5, and 6 focus on the needs of people returning to the church and include suggestions on how to develop programs to meet those needs; Chapter 7 addresses some of the ramifications this ministry will have for the rest of the parish; and Chapter 8 discusses how to begin in your community. The final section of the book contains resource suggestions for further study.

Chapter 1

FEELING CATHOLIC

Our Common Experience

"I'm Catholic." It is a simple sentence that has a great variety of meanings. Sometimes it is spoken with the pride of a new Catholic in the excitement of a first Easter season after full initiation into the Catholic community. Sometimes it sounds more like a battle cry, as different sides argue opinions, each claiming to be more "Catholic" than the other. It is the simple statement of reality for most church members who feel at home and comfortable within their faith. Children show an important sense of maturing faith commitment as they are able to identify themselves as Catholic, and make that statement without prompting.

"I'm Catholic" is also the statement frequently used by some other people—those whom others might have named "inactive" Catholics, "fallen-away" or "lapsed" Catholics. For many of them, the statement remains, "I'm Catholic." It is spoken with ease, almost without thought.

The words somehow contain a hint of a deeper reality, a *feeling* of being Catholic that can be deeper than feelings of anger or alienation. It is a feeling that remains even as one identifies with other faith communities for a time.

Deep inside is the reality, "I'm Catholic." That feeling can become the focus around which ministry to returning Catholics can be developed. Regardless of the forces that led a person away from the community, no matter what the impulse that calls them to consider

3

returning, each one knows the experience of feeling Catholic. That feeling is strong for some and barely noticeable for others, but it is the basic shared experience we have with them. It is that experience or feeling that eventually leads a person back to Catholic friends, or to a Catholic parish community. It is that deep-seated feeling that causes one to respond affirmatively to an invitation to consider returning to their Catholic faith community once again.

Feeling Catholic is not only a beginning point, but it also should be the goal of ministry with returning Catholics. Education can be helpful for them, but that is never enough. Encouraging community and building relationships are essential, but not enough. Liturgical celebrations, however meaningful, will not be enough in themselves. To minister successfully to returning Catholics, one needs to reach the heart, the gut feeling level. A person must once again be brought to the point where he or she *feels* Catholic, and is comfortable with that feeling.

That is what reconciliation means. That is what is expressed in eucharist. That is what ministry to returning Catholics is about.

Meeting the Inactive

Parishes can learn much from the scientific research that has been done in recent years about inactive Catholics. Why they leave, what they are like, what motivates them to consider returning—these are all topics that are covered well in studies, especially by George Gallup and Dean Hoge. A short pamphlet, "Another Look," presents a concise and easy to read summary of those findings. (These references are described in the Resources section at the end of this book.)

Their terminology and insight can be very helpful in planning for local ministry to the inactive. It is also essential to learn personally from the inactive. Because each person's story is unique, the minister must never be satisfied with simply finding the appropriate category for someone. Here are some examples taken from parish experience.

"The Alienated"

One of the largest single groups of inactive Catholics can properly be called "alienated." They have been hurt by the church at some point in their lives (sometimes a real hurt, sometimes an imagined hurt), and they need to reach a point where they can truly forgive and get on with their lives.

> Joyce grew up in the church—literally, she says. Her mother was a housekeeper in a rectory and she spent much of her time there or in the convent. Those church people and places were a safe and comfortable haven during a childhood that often was tumultuous because of an alcoholic and abusive father. In high school she dropped out and married a man who was much like her father. They had two children. Joyce began to realize what was happening in her life, how she was repeating what had happened to her mother. She did not want to be what she was becoming. She turned to her pastor for help. Twenty years ago, his advice was that she should remain faithful to her marriage vows, and make the best of the life she had. At the age of twenty-one, Joyce made a choice that left her alone with two children, isolated even from the church on which she had depended. Her story is remarkable. After twenty years away from the church, Joyce came to a parish program for inactive Catholics with a good friend who is part of the parish. The two of them knew one another well and had shared their spiritual journeys with one another. Joyce trusted her friend enough to give the church another chance.

"Anti-Change Dropouts"

There are "anti-change" Catholics among the inactive. Many who had been very committed and well educated in the church before Vatican II felt that the church left them as the liturgical and other changes swept throughout parishes, too often without there being good preparation or enough accompanying explanation.

> Jim is a policeman in one of the toughest areas of the city. Through much of his day, he is surrounded by people who have given up. Violence, drugs, promiscuity are common-

place. Jim faces these realities with a good traditional Catholic upbringing, and he is not able to integrate the two. He is not comfortable with the changes in the church which appear to him to be a softening or watering down of his faith values or simply making excuses. But he is also not comfortable with himself, as he tries to sustain a value system that doesn't make sense in his life situation. Jim began his serious questioning after making a Marriage Encounter weekend several years ago. He joined a group for returning Catholics in response to an invitation brought home by his son who had just begun in the parish religious education program.

"Too Little Change"

The number of "anti-change" inactives is not a surprise to people, but it often is a surprise that there is just about an equal number of Catholics who have left because of too little change in the church. They are mostly younger people who have been disappointed in the areas where change appears to be needed and has not come.

Anne is a beautiful young woman, married with two small children. Through CCD, attending church, and a strong Catholic family, her memories are those of a solid Catholic upbringing. She tells of remembering her grandmother teaching her "every prayer that had ever been written." Anne stopped coming to church after her marriage. She felt excluded because of her decision about birth control, and chose to leave the problem by leaving the church. She did want her children baptized, however. When she came to the baptism preparation meeting for her second child, she received an invitation to take "Another Look" at her faith. At the first meeting, she described her desire to pass on the best of her faith to her daughters. Even though she had questions and much to work through, she knew there was something drawing her that connected her grandmother, her daughters, and herself.

"Never Committed Catholics"

Many inactive Catholics may properly be called "never-committed Catholics." Often baptized as children, they received some religious training, but were never in a position to make an adult faith commitment. At some point in their lives, they feel drawn to God or the need for a community, and turn to the faith of their early childhood to see if that will satisfy their longing.

Audrey was a baptized Catholic whose Catholic father died when she was twelve years old. After that, she was raised as a member of her mother's Baptist church. She went to her local parish church when she was forty-eight, a wife and mother of four adult children. She shared a longing she had felt throughout her life to re-establish the faith experience she had shared with her father. Audrey had made the decision to go to the parish church because of its reputation for openness to the community. She became part of the Christian initiation process in the parish, and through it returned to membership in the church of her childhood. Over the next several years, one by one, the other members of her family joined her as Catholics. Audrey was exceptional in her ability to tell her story, and was able to share so simply the magnificent actions of God in her life.

The "Active Inactive"

Some inactive Catholics would be called so only by themselves. Externally, they are very much a part of the church, but they feel an emptiness, a yearning for the more that draws them. They do not feel a part of what is going on, and long for a faith that is more integral to their family and community life. They respond to an invitation that says, "Are you not as much a part of the church as you would like to be?"

John showed up at a meeting of returning Catholics because of a notice in the parish bulletin. He regularly read the bulletin—he attended church weekly. He said that in his whole life, he had not missed mass more than three or four times. "I just never knew why I was there," he said. His father was Catholic, his mother was not. Religion was simply never discussed in his family. John, now married and with a son, attends mass every week. He wanted to know why he was coming, and he wanted to tell his son.

"Spiritual Seekers"

Some inactive Catholics are "spiritual seekers." Far from leaving the practice of the faith because of a lack of concern, they left because they were not being fed in their faith community. It was precisely their desire for God that led them to look in other places as they tried to understand more deeply.

> Tim identified himself as an average Catholic. He was fairly regular in his church attendance, but "not a fanatic," he said. Then he began to feel something different. He heard some Bible preachers on the radio. He started to read scripture. He wondered what was happening to him. Tim's wife told him about the group meeting at the parish, and suggested that he try those people for some direction on his journey. Tim now is a leader in parish scripture study, always asking for more opportunity, and ready to share his story of how God found him, and touched him with a powerful hand.

"Family Tension Dropouts"

Some inactive Catholics are called "family tension dropouts." They see the church as part of an old life that has to be left behind. Most often, they are young people who leave the church as part of beginning their new life independent of the family. For others, there are real problems connected with a previous life that are connected to the experience of church for them.

> Tom is a man whose life has taken may turns. He is a Vietnam veteran who has traveled through both drug and alcohol addiction. Through those experiences he has learned God's power and personal care for him. There was

no question about Tom and God; but Tom and the church was a more complicated issue. His wife is an active Catholic, and he wanted to believe, to feel Catholic again, so they could share that part of their lives. But it wasn't easy. Tom has come in and out of groups for returning Catholics. He is able to share his spiritual experiences and listen to others. But he still feels not quite at home in the church. It was part of his old life, he says, and he feels almost fearful as he begins to return to any part of that. Tom stays a beloved and most welcome guest anytime, but he finds his spiritual community primarily through Alcoholic Anonymous at this time.

"Weary Dropouts"

A final category is "weary dropouts," those people who got tired of fighting battles in the church, and tried life without it.

Pam was a rebel all her life. "Even as a child," she said, "I didn't believe all that stuff they were telling me about God." She went through Catholic schools and lived with her traditional Catholic family, scandalizing them regularly by questioning, admitting doubts or brazenly going into church without a hat. She married a man who was not Catholic, and stopped coming to church when they moved to a new neighborhood. Several years later, her father died, and Pam, for the first time in her life, looked beyond the external issues of faith, to find the God who is present in both life and in death. She began a serious spiritual searching, looking for a church group that could satisfy her. She says it was her husband who led her back to the Catholic Church—"If you are going to go to a church, go to a name brand church. I don't want you getting involved with any of those generic ones." She went to her local parish and found companions there. She said it was like finally feeling at home. She was okay here—not a renegade, not a rebel—just Pam, our sister who traveled the journey from death to life, and now shares her gifts with us once again.

An Image from Scripture

Our reaction to inactive Catholics must be in the manner of Jesus, who described himself as the good shepherd. Probably "lost sheep" is not a particularly good term for inactive Catholics. However, "good shepherd" is clearly the right term for the one who cares for them and draws them back. The image of the sheep and the shepherd is filled with the story of God's personal love for each of us.

The shepherd knows the sheep—by name, by sight, by personality. Some sheep are easy to get along with, some are hard. The shepherd and the sheep are interdependent. They eat, live and sleep in close proximity. The shepherd's livelihood is dependent on the sheep; the sheep are not able to survive alone. The community must stay together.

The great danger to a sheep is that it may become "cast"— turned over on its back with no legs touching the ground. If that should happen, the sheep is unable to get up. It would die—without food or water, eventually unable to breathe from its own weight. It is such a danger that sends the shepherd out from the ninety-nine to search for the lost sheep. And indeed it would need to be carried back to the family, where the shepherd will gently massage its legs to get life and strength back into them. You will always find the good shepherd with the one whose need is the greatest.

If we are to minister to inactive Catholics, we much develop the characteristics of a good shepherd. We must know them—personally, as they are. We must be accessible to them. With some, relationships may be easy; with others, connecting will be more difficult. We must remember that we are interdependent. It does matter that we work for unity. As a church, we are not all we should be until we are all together.

Assistance on the journey home, from a good shepherd, is focused on the sheep, to make possible the sheep's return to the fold as a healthy, full member. Being reunited with the sheepfold does not mean blindly following the flock; it is not a gathering where individuality is lost. It is rather being once again part of the community that shares its absolute dependence on the shepherd. That is what identifies the sheep's being truly back home. Ask a shepherd!

Chapter 2

REACHING OUT TO RETURNING CATHOLICS

Personal Invitation

"Would you like to talk about it?"

"Yes, there have been a lot of changes."

"There haven't been that many changes. Deep inside, we really are still the church you knew."

"Maybe you could feel at home in the church again!"

"We miss you."

"We need you."

"Why not come with me to...?"

Issuing the invitation—evangelizing the inactive—has to be the first step in ministry to returning Catholics. Almost fifty percent say they can imagine a situation in which they would at least consider such an invitation. Ninety percent who do join or return to membership in any church do so because they receive such a personal invitation. The statistics are both startling and encouraging.

Parishes serious about ministry to inactive Catholics must find a way to tap the evangelizing potential of its active members. The Catholic Church is called the "sleeping giant of evangelization" by George Gallup. If ever we awakened this giant, what powerful results we could expect! Pope Paul VI, in his apostolic exhortation, "On Evangelization in the Modern World," stated clearly that laity are the primary evangelizers, and, further, that inactive Catholics should be the first beneficiary of our evangelizing activity.

There are two major hurdles to overcome. The first is a complacent parish life that does not challenge its members to evangelize. Evangelization requires an individual with an alive, personal faith that spills over from heart and mind to action and relationships. An evangelizer cannot pretend, cannot intellectualize, cannot rely completely on personal resources. An evangelizer is not a perfect Christian, but is one who has experienced faith in a way that has made a difference in his or her personal life and in the lives of others.

A parish overcomes this obstacle of complacency by seeing itself as a community that provides opportunities for questioning, for sharing faith, for mutual nurturing. It means respecting church members as self-directing adults who experience God in their lives. The goal of adult education, liturgy, Christian initiation, parish renewal programs should be such a personal and communal experience of faith. An evangelizing mentality can be a kind of litmus test for parish formation programs. When one has really heard the good news and been changed by it, that person naturally feels the impulse to share it with others in some way.

The second hurdle has to do with misconceptions about evangelization. A judgmental attitude ("You are not as good as I am"), a heavy-handed approach ("You really have to do this now"), a lack of respect for an individual's unique journey ("My way is the only way") are naturally distasteful for a mature Christian. The word evangelization should not raise such images, but it often does because of some well-publicized bad examples.

Jesus should be our prime model for evangelization. "I have come to bring good news," he said. He offered the invitation to everyone who would listen, and even to those who would not. He spoke a message that was difficult to accept and apply to daily living, yet he did this with honesty and authenticity. But he never forced anyone; he always responded with love and forgiveness, and he spoke with both words and actions.

True Evangelizers

There is a woman named Norma in a large suburban parish who is a model evangelizer. She has three little children and is at home most of the day caring for them. She lives in a neighborhood where much transience and long commutes to places of business translate into loneliness and inpersonalism. But Norma is not like that. She cares about her neighbors. She knows them by name, does favors for them, talks to them and listens to them. The parish staff has gotten used to hearing, in precatechumenate sessions, gatherings for inactive Catholics and over the phone, "I am a neighbor of Norma, one of your members. We were talking the other day, and she suggested I call you about..."

Jeannette is another model evangelizer. She is sixteen years old, a fairly good student, and an active member of her parish youth program. She frequently invites her friends from school to dances, trips and parties at church; she also invites them to retreats, to classes and to Bible study groups. She is known as "one of the Catholic girls" at school, but she is also known as a trusted friend. She was the first to hear of a girlfriend's pregnancy, and she stayed into the night with her, until the friend felt ready to tell her parents. She is often the first to invite a teenager new to the school to become involved in activities. One of her friends has described the effect she had on her in this way: "I saw how important Jeannette's faith was to her, and so I decided to give it a try myself."

If we are to evangelize the inactive in our faith communities, we must tap the evangelizing potential of the ordinary layperson within these communities. We must free from within them the extraordinary charism they possess to share the good news.

Ordinary Parish Life

Almost as a matter of course, the richness of Catholic parish life can be a tremendous evangelizing tool. While it requires little additional effort, it must be a focused effort, accompanied by a cooperative spirit among parish leaders.

Preparing for a Child's Baptism

Interviews and sessions for parents of children to be baptized are prime occasions for evangelization. The birth of a child is one of those "crisis events" Dean Hoge identifies as a facilitating event for evangelization. The sense of hope we feel for this new life touches even the hardest heart with the desire to be good. Every parent wants to give good example for the child, to be a good parent, to protect this child in every way possible.

Obviously, parishes need to build on the positive and avoid the negative possibilities surrounding baptism preparation. For instance, no one should be told "NO" over the phone, when calling about a baptism. While it may be true that the baptism will not be able to happen how and when the caller wants it, or on the caller's conditions, that hard message must always be given in the context of a personal and understanding encounter.

The liturgical experience of baptism must not become an impersonal event that appears to be empty ritual. Even when many babies are baptized the same day, the sacrament demands that we not forget the individual. The water is not indiscriminately tossed out at people, it is lovingly poured to surround *this* child with our God's saving power. Remembering each baby's name, including gentle touching and rich symbol use, giving gifts that the family gets to keep, makes a family know "This was *my* baby's baptism."

Of course, most parishes work to make baptism preparation helpful and good. They see it as a chance for family and adult formation, and they expend considerable energy in making baptism a positive experience. But even where the program is a good one, the evangelizing potential can be lost. Ask yourself these questions:

Does the program leader pay attention to subtle signs of a parent's desire to feel at home in church once again? Is there a spirit of invitation to other opportunities for growth in faith, rather than an attempt to satisfy all questions in this one program? Does your parish have programs to recommend where continuing searching is not only possible, but welcome? Does the baptism preparation leader know about them? Are fliers available that advertise programs for returning Catholics and those who are interested in becoming Catholic? Is there any help with child care for parents with small children who may be interested in these programs? Are names and phone numbers of those with some interest in returning to the church shared with parish leaders more directly involved with evangelization?

A Need for Exceptions

How do you handle the really tough cases? It is seldom that a family absolutely refuses to come to any preparation sessions. (Many may need extra cajoling and encouragement, but at least they come.) A commitment to evangelization would call for the possibility for some alternative. Could you go to them? It would take them by surprise, but probably a family would agree to a personal visit. Consider these two cases from parish experience. In each one, the parents were adamant about objecting to parish requirements for baptism preparation. As a compromise, the parish minister arranged a personal interview in the home to talk about it.

In one case, it turned out that the child was illegitimate, and the mother was embarrassed to come to such a meeting with families. The visit allowed the parish to begin the special ministry she needed to help her prepare for her role as a single parent. She needed a support group and friends—and the church—more than many others who face parenthood.

The other family was a second generation in a family that was a long-time pillar of the church. They couldn't comprehend that there would be any question about baptizing their child. The personal visit began amid some hostility, but ended positively, as the couple did enjoy the anticipation of the baby's baptism. They also recognized the stubbornness they had exhibited in refusing to meet with anyone. They said, "Thanks for coming."

Preparing for Other Sacraments

Preparation programs for parents who want their children to receive eucharist, confirmation, and reconciliation offer the same kind of potential for evangelization. Such parent meetings are often the largest educational gatherings for adults in a parish. It is so important to make the most of them.

For instance, so many parents start out asking about children wearing white for first communion. Our reaction can range from ridiculing the question ("Clothes are not that important; white veils went out with the fast from midnight") to building on the parents' memories of faith experiences, and helping them see how they can help their children have solid faith experiences ("Do you remember what you wore for first communion? How did it make you feel? What kind of feelings do you hope for your child? How can you encourage those feelings for them?").

In any such gathering of parents, the leader should expect a group that represents what pastoral experience suggests is average for the whole church — one third active parishioners, one third semi-active, and one third inactive. Such a gathering provides a prime opportunity to offer a solid, loving, helpful program that can be, in itself, an invitation to explore one's level of trust in the church. Such meetings should start with parents where they are, and help them move to the next step. Assuming too much— that they are at ease with theological questions, or that they have personalized and reflected upon their faith—can make the presentation incomprehensible. Challenging them to move too far or too fast—to replace all old symbols with new ones—causes a defensive attitude that alienates rather than reconciles.

Family Gatherings Associated with the Church

Wakes, funerals and weddings are other normal parts of parish life that offer clear opportunities to reach inactive Catholics. They are present for those family gatherings, often expecting to feel unwelcome or put down. If, instead, they are welcomed warmly, if the flow of the liturgy is gentle and clear, if there is a personal touch, a handshake, an introduction offered, then inactive Catholics may experience a true call to reconsider their own feelings toward the church.

Making the sacrament of reconciliation available after wakes or wedding rehearsals is a practical step that often has immediate results, if the announcement is non-threatening, and the confessor gentle.

Sunday Liturgy

Our most significant action as church is our celebration of Sunday liturgy. This too can and should be an evangelizing event. Are people welcome there? Of course, it is easy to "say" yes—but do we "act" yes? How does someone know what time masses are? Is there an outdoor sign that says "Welcome"? Are there people who say "Welcome" as greeters or ushers or ministers of hospitality? Do members of the assembly make room for newcomers or returnees—room in the pew, and room in the community? Is the liturgy simple and clear? Do the symbols speak with power? Will a new person be drawn into the action by the power of the action itself? Challenge your liturgy planners to think about liturgy as an evangelizing event.

Christmas and Easter

Take advantage of the Christmas and Easter crowds. During Lent and Advent, prepare regular churchgoers for the evangelizing potential of those days. Will you crowd into the pews with a welcoming smile? Will you sincerely greet the person next to you, and assist in that person's participation? Will you offer the few extra minutes for hospitality before and after mass? Evangelizing communities should have special advertisements and invitations prepared for those days, to take advantage of the few but very real and viable occasions that still connect us to those who are otherwise absent. [See Figure1.]

Support Staff

A final part of ongoing parish life to consider is your parish secretary, or the person who answers the phone and greets visitors. The influence that person has on the evangelization efforts of a parish cannot be overestimated. Sooner or later, just about every person drawn to your church will encounter this person, and often that will be the first formal contact.

Consider the stories of two separate parishes. In one there was a secretary who clearly saw her job as a ministry of welcome. She attended workshops on evangelization, and as a parishioner volunteered to be a sponsor for a catechumen, and later as a team member for returning Catholics. She answered each phone call and greeted each visitor with more than a good secretary's ability. She was a channel of the Spirit for those people. She recalls how, on a few occasions, she would be dealing with a very difficult person and have to remind herself that this person might just be ripe to experience God's call to our community.

The other extreme was a parish that had no secretary. The door and phone were answered by a housekeeper who really was overworked. The parish made a real effort to reach out to the neighbors, but often when they responded by reaching out to that parish, they would hear, "He's busy now," or "We can't be taking care of everybody, you know."

Look at your secretary's job description. Is it to protect the pastor...to weed out moochers...to decide who gets appointments with

_____ I have questions about the Catholic Church, and would like to talk with someone about them.

_____ I have been away from the Catholic Church for awhile, and would like to talk with someone about coming back.

_____ I am not Catholic, and would like to talk with someone about becoming a Catholic.

_____ I would like more information about _____ _____. Please have someone call me.

✦ ✦ ✦ ✦

Name: _____

Address:_____

Phone:_____

Please place this form in the collection, or in one of the baskets at the entrances of the Church.
Someone will be in touch with you within a few weeks.

Figure 1. This text could be used on two halves of a folded invitation on either Christmas or Easter. The front of the invitation could include art appropriate to the season and perhaps the world "Welcome!" to spark interest.

whom? Or is it to help the parish staff communicate more effectively...to be an initial sign of the welcome to be expected in this community?

Using Specific Evangelization Outreach

This chapter has so far talked about the ongoing mentality of evangelization that should pervade parish life. With just a little effort and really no extra funds, a parish can successfully evangelize in these ways. Eventually, however, as a parish becomes serious about evangelization and begins to taste its fruit, it will be ready to reach out in more planned programs of evangelization to the inactive in the community.

Have Parishioners Identify Inactive Friends or Neighbors

One successful method has been to ask active parishioners to identify their friends or neighbors who are inactive. This outreach is best done as part of a weekend focus at liturgies on reaching out to our inactive friends, neighbors, and family. At all weekend masses, the homilies describe some of the causes of alienation or inactivity, and describe parish services for those who consider themselves to be inactive or alienated.

An attractive invitation flier is available at the doors of the church. It invites people who have been away from the church to consider taking "Another Look" at what it means to be Catholic. It promises "no obligation, no pressure." Parishioners are encouraged to take one to hand-deliver to a friend or relative, and to add a personal invitation to "Come with me to the first few weeks." For those who feel uncomfortable with that personal action, they can choose to write down the name and address of their friend and an invitation will be mailed. If a phone number is included, a member of the evangelization team will call with an invitation to the parish program for returnees. [See Figure 2.]

Such a program as this is best done every two or three years rather than annually, so it maintains a freshness in the community. In a parish of two thousand families, one could expect about four hundred invitations to be taken by parishioners, about seventy-five names to be

DID YOU GO TO A CATHOLIC SCHOOL
and have stories to tell?

WERE YOU RAISED CATHOLIC
but do not come to Church anymore?

ARE YOU A CATHOLIC
who now feels separated from your Church?

**WOULD YOU LIKE TO KNOW MORE ABOUT THE CHURCH
AS IT IS TODAY?**

**WOULD YOU LIKE TO FEEL AT HOME IN THE CATHOLIC
CHURCH AGAIN?**

_____
(name of parish)

invites you to take
ANOTHER LOOK

ANOTHER LOOK is a series of get-togethers concerning topics of interest to people who have been away from the Church for some time. It is a chance for you to talk about your experiences. What was it like for you? Were you hurt by Church rules in the past? Do you have a problem with confession? Do you wonder about changes in the Church?

TAKE THE FIRST STEP! Accept this invitation to begin to talk about yourself and the Catholic Church. You will be glad you did it!

MEETINGS BEGIN SOON

_____
(indicate proposed day and time)

Meetings will be held at _____.
For more information, call_____ at
_____.

The program is free. There is no obligation.
LET'S TALK ABOUT IT!

Figure 2. Invitation flier to take "Another Look."

submitted for mailed invitations, and about forty phone numbers given for a team member to call.

Use Parish and Local Media

Newspaper stories and advertisements reach many inactive Catholics. The stories are free, and can be good public relations for the parish as well as an effective method of evangelization for inactive Catholics. Telling the stories of people who have made the journey back to active membership is especially effective.

Signs in front of your church are often overlooked, but can be so important. Do you let people know they are welcome? When you are concentrating on reaching the inactive, can your sign say that? Is there a billboard available in your parish area? Use it!

Invite the Bishop to Help

Another outreach program that was successful involved inviting a local bishop to assist the parish in reaching out to the inactive. A meeting was scheduled with the bishop and parish leaders to hear from inactive Catholics. Outdoor signs, posters and community newspapers all shared the bold invitation: "Inactive Catholics—Tell the Bishop Why."

No one knew what to expect! Seventeen people responded by attending the meeting. After one half hour of informal sharing with refreshments, there was one hour when each person had time to tell his or her story. The bishop and the parishioners listened. The bishop commented briefly in response, offered compassion and support, and made notes. No one attempted to take care of everything at that moment. Each person was invited to some follow-up, and most responded to those invitations. The final half hour had more individual sharing in which parishioners and staff entered into personal conversations with the participants.

The meeting was good in itself, but it had a surprise lasting result as well. Since then, several people have come to the parish because of the publicity surrounding that meeting. Such a public event effectively promoted the parish's reputation as a listening, welcoming place.

Such one-time events have limited effect in themselves, but when combined with several other welcoming messages, they can provide the groundwork that brings a person to the point of taking some positive action toward the church.

Personal Touch

The only way to be sure to invite every inactive Catholic in your community is to reach out door-to-door. Personal knocking on doors remains a mainstay of evangelization, but one that requires much time and a long-term commitment. It can be done, however, and is well worth the effort. A parish in Pennsylvania has just completed their ten-year plan for staff visitation of every home in the community. A few hours were spent each week by each staff member, following a well-defined map for parish coverage. Their experience made the decision to begin again an easy one!

A parish can also touch each door through fliers or handbills left at each home, or, through mailed information, it can use the local mail carrier as an agent of evangelization.

The Paulist National Catholic Evangelization Association offers an excellent program for this method of evangelization. *Information From* is a six page tabloid delivered to every home in a zip code area of your choosing. Your parish is pictured on the masthead (i.e. *Information From...St. Joseph's Parish*). The tabloid contains stories about family life, personal development and Christian lifestyles. One whole page is left open for local use, to advertise your parish schedule and the services/activities available. The paper is delivered six times a year, and builds a strong welcoming reputation for your parish community. It is recommended that the local Protestant churches and your own church members be advised about the program, with the assurance that its purpose is to reach the inactive and unchurched, and not to challenge one's personal active faith. The cost of this program is about one dollar per address per year, with a minimum of two thousand addresses in the zip code area chosen. For details write to Paulist National Catholic Evangelization Association, 3031 Fourth Street N.E. Washington, D.C. 20017.

Your parish will be able to discover still more ways of reaching out to the inactive. Experience breeds creativity. In a very real sense, we need to believe that it is impossible to fail in this work. So long as our invitation is offered with love and respect for freedom, it will be an experience of God's love for the person. If the person rejects the invitation, he or she has still been touched. If the person accepts the invitation, so much the better. Either way, we who have evangelized have been the channel of God's grace; *we* have been touched as well.

Chapter 3

PROGRAMMING FOR RETURNING CATHOLICS IN YOUR PARISH

In the Spirit of Christian Initiation

Good ministry to returning Catholics just begins with the invitation. Almost all people who have experienced separation from the church and now feel drawn to reconciliation with the community need and want something to help in that process. Some people do not choose anything other than sacramental reconciliation, and we must respect that choice. It remains our right and privilege as Catholics. Participation in any other process is usually helpful, but only when it is freely chosen.

Many parishes choose to invite returning Catholics into sessions planned for those joining the church in the process of Christian initiation. It is true that there are many similarities between the needs of catechumens or candidates and returning Catholics. However, there are also many basic differences. With only rare exceptions, returning Catholics are better served in a separate group that supports a process similar to Christian initiation, rather than in a group mixed with catechumens and candidates. Those who are programming for returning Catholics need to understand what needs are similar, and learn from our experience with Christian initiation. But they also need to identify where needs are different, and address them specifically. And, finally, it is important for them to recognize those exceptions in which a returning Catholic may be better served by joining with catechumens and candidates for reception into full communion.

The similarities are these: (1) What is offered must be more process than program; (2) it is adult in nature; (3) companions for the journey are essential; (4) it takes time; (5) rituals are needed to express what is happening; (6) good catechesis is required.

1. More Process Than Program

What you design must be more process than program. The determining factor in what actually happens at a given time is not the program you have planned, but what is happening for the people involved. That means you do have a program planned. Schedules and space are on the parish calendar. There is a lesson plan for the evening, and a desired outcome. But those plans and that program must be attentive to what is actually happening for participants. Insights emerge that cannot be planned; examples from the lives of participants affirm the basic reality of God or church; questions that arise call leaders as well as members to deeper reflection and discovery. That is the Holy Spirit. That is process.

Planning for it requires well-prepared group leaders, regular prayer—both individually and as a community—and a gift for sensitivity to God's movement within. We must program, but the program is always the servant of the conversion process. God is the one in charge.

2. Adult in Nature

People involved in this process are adults and must absolutely be treated as such. This may sound simple, but often it is hard to achieve. For many adults, especially those over forty, experience in the church often has not been an adult experience. Before Vatican II, our church was "Holy Mother Church" and the hierarchy was unquestionably "Father." We were the children—called to obedience and cautioned against questioning.

While much has happened to change these characterizations for today, we should not judge the past too harshly. It was not only the church that treated adults as less than adults. That was the way the nation treated its citizens, an industry treated its workers, a teacher treated students. That was the society of the past, and while the church must certainly move beyond the past to the present, it is not productive to condemn its past as all bad.

To say that returning Catholics must be treated as adults assumes parish leaders who are ready and able to do that. In most cases, that is not the problem. The problem often lies in the returning Catholic. It is hard to accept the responsibilities of adulthood in the faith. In many cases, the person is happy to hear that the church no longer requires this or that; but that same person is not so happy to hear that he or she can no longer settle for just following the rules. For instance, it seems like good news that the church no longer requires daily fast and abstinence during Lent; yet it is hard to hear the news that each person is called during Lent to scrutinize the personal use of material things, and adjust one's behavior in light of the gospel message.

Adults have past experiences and memories which, whether good or bad, must be recognized and accepted if there is to be movement. Adults are responsible for themselves whether they want to be or not. Adults will choose to whom they will listen, and what they will believe. Scripture and church history remind us that God has always treated us as adults. We cannot attempt to be anything less than adults.

3. A Need for Companions

Companions are needed for the journey. Because human beings need one another; because a faith journey calls for serious life decisions; because when God calls a person, that person is always called to community; because individualism is one of the special temptations today that we must resist: we need others with whom to make our journey.

Some of those companions will be other returning Catholics who share their experiences. Some will be team members who develop relationships with participants. Some will be special friends or relatives who journey with the returning Catholic.

4. It Takes Time

As with any meaningful process, the journey takes time, and should not be rushed or delayed. People involved in any conversion process are involved in making changes, and any change takes time. Doing something once is not enough. Alcoholics Anonymous has a saying, "If nothing changes—nothing changes." Time is required to help people test out new ways of being who they are. They need time to practice, time to develop new habits, so that something really has the chance to change inside.

Time is also needed to really forgive and to let bitterness subside. For many returning Catholics the most significant thing to happen is their gradual movement to honestly let go of hurts they experienced in the past in the church. Unless that forgiveness on their part is sincere, their journey cannot be complete. Freedom from the bonds of past hurts is necessary for a person to be an active adult member of the community. That kind of healing requires time.

5. A Need for Ritual

Ritual is our community's way of expressing what is most real and most human in our experience. The deepest realities of life call for expression in a symbol language that says more than words ever could. Baptism says what is most true about death and new life; marriage says what is most true about love and self-giving; eucharist says what is most true about our community and God's presence in it. Reconciliation must speak clearly what is most true about a person's return to the community, and the freedom, salvation, and forgiveness that come with it.

The ritual of reconciliation is not contained exclusively in the moment of sacramental reconciliation. There can and should be ritual moments leading to that experience in the same way that the liturgical stages of Christian initiation lead to baptism, confirmation and eucharist. (Further discussion on the role of ritual for the returning Catholic occurs in Chapter 6.)

6. Good Catechesis

A final similarity between Christian initiation and ministry to returning Catholics is the need for excellent catechesis. Catechesis is a technical term whose meaning must be understood in its fullest sense. Catechesis is not a series of lectures, no matter how good the content. It is not dependent on a text, no matter how complete it is. It is not contained in a videotape no matter how professional its production.

Catechesis is echoing, resounding, sharing faith. It happens person to person, though it may use texts or media or guest speakers. It happens in the context of a community, though personal study is important. It challenges participants to action and direct service. It always inspires prayer and worship. Catechesis includes message, community, service and worship. Returning Catholics need such catechesis. (Chapter 4 looks at that need in depth.)

Differences from Christian Initiation

There are four major areas where returning Catholics differ from catechumens and candidates: they are Catholic, they have experiences and memories that form their understanding of the church, they have more extensive relationships to Catholic groups—their family, school friends, priests, sisters, parish leaders, etc., and the focus of their journey is reconciliation, not initiation. These four characteristics should influence all the programming designed for returning Catholics.

The starting point is Catholic memory and experiences rather than the fresh view of one just moving toward church membership. Learning experiences must always begin with remembered past teachings and connect those with the presentation. There often needs to be some "un-learning" involved. That is usually not needed for new Catholics. In a sense, for returning Catholics, the journey starts with Catholic, moves to Christian, then back to Catholic Christian. In Christian initiation it starts with Christian and moves to Catholic Christian.

Christian initiation is a liturgical process, related to the liturgical year that reaches its highpoint in the celebration of baptism, confirmation and eucharist at the Easter vigil, with continuing experiences throughout the Easter season. Ministry with returning Catholics is less tied to liturgical seasons and is not currently guided by church documents for its process. While adequate time is needed for the experience, it is usually not as long a time as is needed for the process of Christian initiation.

While similarities with Christian initiation are many, the differences call for a separate experience for returning Catholics. Such a separation assures proper attention not only to the returning Catholic, but also to the catechumen and candidate. When other groups are included with them, it usually requires enough adjustments that the catechumen and candidate end up missing out on the attention they deserve.

There are a few cases where a returning Catholic is properly invited to sessions for those in the process of Christian initiation: (1) when the person is baptized but truly uncatechized, that is, not formed in the faith at all; usually, this means that the person has not received Eucharist. (The Rite of Christian Initiation of Adults, Chapter 4, Part II, addresses this situation specifically); the person is called to the initiation sacraments of confirmation and eucharist; (2) when the person was truly never committed to the faith, even as a child (i.e. someone who really has no substantial church memories at all); (3) when the returning Catholic is a spouse of a current catechumen or candidate, and requests participation with the spouse in the process of Christian initiation rather than the process for returning Catholics.

Parish Programs for Returning Catholics

It is left to each individual parish to bring to life the structure that will use the gifts in its community to effectively serve the needs of returning Catholics in its area. The program descriptions that follow may be helpful in getting started or in helping your parish programs to grow. The first is described in greatest detail for the purpose of giving an in-depth look at one parish's experience.

Another Look (St. Joseph Parish, Sykesville, Maryland)

(The name ANOTHER LOOK is borrowed from the Paulist National Catholic Evangelization Association. It is the name of their personalized mail outreach to inactive Catholics. The parish program is not connected to that. The name was chosen because it so aptly describes what participants are invited to do—they take ANOTHER LOOK at what it means to be Catholic.)

There is a leadership team of three to five people including one staff person. At the beginning of each season, evangelization efforts have gathered about eight to fifteen people interested in ANOTHER LOOK. Meetings for this group are scheduled at the same time as those for Christian initiation and the children's catechumenate sessions. Often members of families are involved in those other groups. There is also the added benefit of the opportunity to share refreshment time among all three groups, which can broaden the awareness of the forms of the conversion journey.

The first week's meeting is spent entirely on getting to know one another, and beginning to identify those areas of question, hurt, confusion or interest. People's comments are listed by a team member—wherever possible using the exact words. It often takes great effort to avoid answering or discussing those issues on the spot. It is important to simply list them so that they can be dealt with in context at a later time. Another reason for just hearing the issues is that you have then heard and accepted not only the issue, but also each person. Even those whose expressions were angry or extreme are welcome to come back. The issue is cared for by being written down; the person is cared for by an unshaken acceptance from the team no matter what is said.

When time allows on the first night, there is also an experience to open some "right brain" church memories, by using a centering exercise. The participants are asked to recall an early clear memory of the church. After time to smell. . .hear . . .see. . .and feel. . .the participants are invited to describe that memory. This usually helps the team understand each person in a deeper way as plans for future sessions are developed. What they remember and the way it is shared is more telling about their real Catholic feelings than are their questions.

Later that week, the team designs a suggested curriculum for the ensuing ten weeks or so. That curriculum is presented at the second meeting, along with time for additional questions and adjustments the group may request. It is important that the curriculum include the specific issues as worded by the participants. Under a heading like "The Mass Today" would be questions like "Why do people talk in church?" "Why is there so much singing?" "Where is the tabernacle?"

Questions about birth control, confession and mortal/venial sin can be handled after a discussion of adult conscience formation, the meaning of sacrament today, and the challenge of social justice. People are willing to wait for their specific issue when they see it on paper!

Each of the following weeks covers a topic that combines several of the issues they raised, along with the areas the team believes they need to consider in looking at the church today. There are three elements to each session: people describe their current understanding of the issue; there is a presentation of the church's practice in that area today; finally, there are questions or discussions about the effect this has on one's personal life. (This is the shared Christian praxis method of adult education: sharing one's personal story and vision, presenting the Master Story and Vision which is the story and vision of Jesus and the church, then applying the new Vision to our old vision.)

During the program the team strives to informally divide up the participants so that each one has a special relationship with one of the team members. The returning Catholics are encouraged to begin coming to mass regularly if they are not already doing so, with the recommendation that they sit with a team member or another friend when they come.

Toward the end of the group's time together, there is a session on the local parish community. The team strives to facilitate connections for the returning Catholic with an ongoing parish group as well as some opportunity for service, where appropriate.

Sacramental reconciliation is usually described about the sixth or seventh week, and at that point there is the promise of an opportunity for reconciliation at the end of ANOTHER LOOK for those who wish to participate. By the last week, the team is able to design a reconciliation service that can ritually express what has happened to the group. It is vital that the service allow participation at various levels. Those not yet ready for full sacramental reconciliation are still welcome to participate and express the reconciliation that has grown in their lives. The evening ends with a celebration, of course. Most people by then are involved in some ongoing part of parish life. Usually a few people are not finished yet. Some will choose to return to the next ANOTHER LOOK group; some will move to a more personal journey with a sponsor, friend or a spiritual director.

Re-Membering Church (a national training program)

The North American Forum on the Catechumenate offers training for parish teams ministering to returning Catholics. Many parishes who have had leaders trained in this way call their parish program by the same name.

The training is experiential and helps each person know the meaning of companionship and the value of ritual. Through presentations on the causes of alienation or separation from the church, the program enables teams to understand the variety of needs among returning Catholics. The study of the sacrament of reconciliation is particularly helpful in designing experiences that can express the richness of the sacrament for people.

These sessions generally promote ministry with inactive Catholics following the liturgical year, and hold out the vision of a revised Order of Penitents with celebrations on Ash Wednesday and Holy Thursday. The desired experience is not one of condemnation of the returning Catholic, but rather the effect on the rest of the community that calls the whole church into a penitential season, and a celebration of a "Return to the Table of Prophets and Witnesses" on Holy Thursday.

For more information on this program, write to the North American Forum on the Catechumenate, 5510 Columbia Pike, Suite 310, Arlington, VA 22204.

Reaching Out to Inactive Catholics (Rev. William McKee, CSSR)

This short book, published in 1980 by Liguori Publications, presented the first example of parishes reaching out specifically to alienated Catholics. Father McKee describes a weekend where there is a strong guest homilist at all masses, followed by a week of catechetical sessions to respond to the questions of inactive Catholics who attend. He describes various methods of helping participants raise those questions in a supportive community, and the importance of a follow-up on future evenings that responds to the spoken and unspoken questions and needs.

His work is based on years of experience as such a guest homilist and the leader for the follow-up sessions. His words clearly exhibit the gentle spirit needed in ministry with returning Catholics.

Retreats, Mini-Missions

Some parishes have taken the direction of a shorter, more intense program for inactive Catholics. Rev. Joseph Breighner in the archdiocese of Baltimore has developed a mini-mission, a four day preaching program for parishes with the goal of reaching and reconciling inactive Catholics. The first night is geared to active parishioners, who are challenged to bring an inactive friend or relative for future evenings. Each of the following nights includes a good and inspiring message, along with an opportunity for reconciliation after the program.

Retreat houses may offer a weekend retreat experience for inactive Catholics. Those who would commit to a full weekend are already far along on their journey, however, and so recruitment is a major part of the planning for such an event.

Spiritual growth activities sponsored for the whole parish—like days of recollection, prayer breakfasts, missions or retreats — can often also serve as a means of reaching inactive Catholics. To make such parish events truly inviting for inactive Catholics would require some extra planning, and some leaders who could concentrate on the specific needs of the person who has been away from the church for a while.

How Will Your Parish Begin?

Chapter 8 gives some general guidelines about getting started. The challenge suggested by this chapter on programming is that of visualizing the structures that might be most effective in your parish community.

If your community is experienced in Christian initiation ministry, build on that to begin a ministry to returning Catholics. If you are able to find a dynamic homilist or mission preacher who can spearhead your efforts, build on that foundation. If your community is blessed with available spiritual directors or retreat centers, consider the use of those builidng blocks.

The way you begin will not be your final plan. All ministry, but most certainly evangelizing ministry, needs flexibility, creativity and diversity. Learn from the models mentioned here, talk with anyone you can find in your diocese who has experience, and use your parish community's best methods of planning.

Then, expect to learn, regroup and improve with every experience you have. There is not *one* way to minister to returning Catholics. The program you design is "right" if it allows God's grace free rein!

Chapter 4

CATECHETICAL NEEDS OF RETURNING CATHOLICS

Recognizing the Need

Educational programs by themselves may attract an inactive Catholic, but education by itself will never be enough. More often, advertisements for adult religious education will not even reach the conscious level for someone alienated from the church. Yet people who are considering a return to church membership clearly express a need to learn, a desire for information, a movement toward discussing and experiencing anew one's faith and belief.

For those who have been inactive because of "the changes" or the lack of changes, or who have been away for a long time because of family concerns or lifestyle, or just apathy, the questioning and searching for knowledge are foremost. Questions are formulated easily, and one of the leadership's challenges is to make it clear to *them* that it is not only information that is needed.

For others—those alienated because of some past or current hurt suffered—knowledge is less a priority. However, the discussion, community support, and reminders of the faith we share do help those returning Catholics as well. The team must be aware of the courage and openness exhibited by such people in even presenting themselves for any program in the church. Their willingness to listen and to open up to others marks a long first step in their possible reconciliation with the church. Their situation reminds *us* that it is not only information that is needed.

Just as in planning the catechumenate in the process of Christian initiation, the team must remember the limits of information, and the many other things needed beyond information, but they must also recognize the need for excellent learning experiences for adults on a conversion journey. Adults need accurate information to be freed to make personal choices, to act as adults, to be able to affirm or reject one's faith or one's faith community.

What Do They Want To Hear? What Do They Need To Hear?

Some issues will always be raised by the group. At least one person will voice it, and most others affirm it as their own:

Birth Control—Can I be in the church and still practice birth control? What right does the church have to tell me how many children I should have?

Divorce and Annulments—Why can't I receive the sacraments? What happens to the children when a marriage is annulled? How much does it cost? Why is the church concerned with marriages of non-Catholics?

Conscience Formation—How can it be that one priest says one thing and another priest says something else? How do you tell what is a sin nowadays?

Changes in the Mass—I don't know what is happening now. I feel uncomfortable. Where is the reverence that used to be so important?

Raising Children in the Church—Why do I have to go to meetings about baptism or first communion? Why don't my children learn the way I did?

Sacraments (Reconciliation in Particular)—Do I have to go to confession? I had a bad experience with confession. Why should I have to talk to a man?

Clearly these issues need attention in whatever program is designed. There are other issues that should be included as well, even though they may not be raised immediately by the returning Catholic. They include scripture, prayer, the need for community, images of

God, the development of the church through history, and social justice issues.

There are questions about those topics, but frequently they may not be the initial questions raised. Someone on the team can encourage those topics with a statement like, "Do you have any feelings about the Bible and the Catholic Church?" Then specific questions from the group can be formulated, and those topics as well become part of the curriculum. When an important issue just has not been raised by the group, the team can still add it to the curriculum, with the explanation that it really seems important. The group should still get to okay the curriculum, though, and if they really do not want to discuss a certain issue, it should be eliminated.

Sample Curriculum

Here is a sample curriculum used in one parish. (The topic headings are the words of the team. The questions and statements under them are in the words of the participants. The items in bold were those the team had to encourage or add on its own.)

Prayer

> What does it mean to pray?
> How can we grow in our prayer life?
> **Images of God**

What Is the Church?

> How did the church make the changes?
> **What are images for the church?**
> Whose rules are these?
> Have there really been any changes?
> Did we misunderstand, or was the church wrong?
> What about women's involvement in the church today?

What Will Be My Personal Experience of the Church Now?

> Why are there inconsistencies from area to area?
> What's okay and what's not okay?

The altar is gone; I can't follow in my missal; it all seems so
foreign.

Authority and Conscience

Sin and fear were so much a part of my life
Birth control issues
How do I know what's okay and what's not okay?

Sin and Forgiveness

What is sin?
Why can't I go directly to God for forgiveness?

Sacraments (Especially Reconciliation)

Do we still believe in sacraments?
Why do we need a middleman?
What does the church teach about inter-communion?
What is confession like today?

Marriage and Family Life

Why won't the church accept divorce?
Marriage regulations today
Family relationships and how the church impacts them

Scripture

Are the stories really true?
Which Bible do we use now?
What did the author really mean to say?

Social Justice

Social agencies and charities
The church and money

Curriculum Elements

The program plan or curriculum that a parish develops to help returning Catholics should contain all these elements:

1. It should make clear ties to the past. There are few, if any, genuinely new things in our church today. Showing changes as developments or moving back to basics is an especially important part of presenting material for returning Catholics.

2. It should prepare the person for change. The church as it is today is not finished and one true constant is the reality of change. Parish leaders today can be tempted to simply replace old absolutes with new absolutes. One may prefer the new, but the reality is that neither old nor new is an absolute.

3. It must challenge each person as much as he or she can take, but no more. A very important lesson for leaders in this ministry is that returning Catholics do not have to end up like them. Some will come through the whole process, and still really not like holding hands at the Our Father. That is okay. There are many Catholics who feel that way. Some may remain quite traditional in their devotions, their views toward political activism, or their feelings about community. That is okay. There are many Catholics who feel that way.

4. Leaders need to speak the truth in love. But each person remains free to hear and respond in his or her own manner. They need to feel comfortable with differences in the church. So do the program leaders.

Encouraging Ongoing Learning

All returning Catholics need to know how to keep updated in their faith. Each should certainly subscribe to the diocesan newspaper if the parish does not make it available. Help them understand how to use it and interpret it. Make available copies of other Catholic periodicals, and encourage them to subscribe to one of them (e.g. *Our Sunday Visitor, America, Catholic World, U.S. Catholic,* etc.).

Promote their personal ongoing Bible study by showing them how to use a resource like *Share the Word* or *God's Word Today.* Make sure they have a good translation of the Bible for personal use.

Provide copies of at least one pastoral from either the National

Conference of Catholic Bishops or the United States Catholic Conference and/or a copy of a pastoral letter from your own bishop.

Make sure they know how to interpret what they read, and where to get answers when they have questions.

See the section at the end of this book for these and other referenes. Several books are described that can be helpful in ministry to returning Catholics as well.

Some Teaching Techniques That Have Worked

Using a Time Line

Time lines are extremely helpful to highlight development and show connections. Consider using the same time line over several weeks to mark the major points in the growth of scripture and the history of the church. [See Figure 3 for a sample.] Make sure to extend the time line into the future, and have participants discuss what might be coming and when. As they raise an issue, help them understand what would have to happen for the change to occur. They will surely raise issues like married priests (which would require a change in a law the church made for itself) and women priests (which would require a change in a basic theological interpretation of scripture and tradition). Help them also look into the future of ecumenism (what might lie ahead in developing church unity?), parish staffing (share the reality of priestless parishes), the place of the third world in the church, and other current issues for your community.

Where Are You on the Spectrum?

Seeing the wide spectrum of Catholicism is important. On one or several issues, individuals can be invited to place themselves (x) and this parish (y) on a spectrum. [See Figure 4.]

On the spectrum of transcendence versus imminence, beware of *either* seeing God as so distant that there is no involvement in our lives, *or* as so comfortable a part of our lives that God becomes a "warm fuzzy." Anywhere on the spectrum is okay, but you can fall off either edge into "not okay."

On the spectrum of the mass as personal prayer versus the mass as community prayer, beware of *either* shutting out the rest of the as-

Left timeline (A.D.):

- **0**
- **33** — Death and resurrection
- **45** — Paul's Letters
- **75** — Early gospels
- **100** — Gospel of John
- **150** — 4 gospels circulated together; "catholic" epistles added
- **200** — term "New Testament" used; canon fixed
- **400** — Vulgate translation
- **800** — Copies of scripture by hand; chapter and verse numbers added
- **1415** — Printing press; Bible first book printed
- **1575** — King James translation to English
- **1940** — Dead Sea Scrolls
- **1965** Vatican II's Dogmatic Constitution Divine Revelation
- **1970** — New American Bible
- **1993**

Right timeline (B.C.):

- **1800 B.C.** — Abraham
- **1280 B.C.** — Moses, desert experiences, Passing on of stories
- **1000 B.C.** — David, Time of peace philosophy, writing down of stories
- **587 B.C.** — Babylonian captivity
- **538 B.C.** — understanding prophets
- **336 B.C.** — Alexander the Great, Septuagint
- **200 B.C.** — Maccabees and other books not included in King James Version
- **0** — Birth of Jesus

Figure 3. Time lines.

God is transcendent, distant, in heaven	_____	God is imminent, close, always near
The mass is a special time for my personal prayer	_____	The mass is a special time for community prayer
I am most comfortable, with the old ways of the church	_____	I am most comfortable with the changes and new ways in the church

Figure 4. Spectrum. Consider the issues and mark "x" for where you are on the spectrum and "y" for where your parish is on the spectrum.

sembly so that we pretend to be alone, *or* of not feeling any responsibility for entering personally into the prayer of the mass.

On the spectrum of the old ways versus the new ways, beware of *either* closing off any possibility of change, *or* of ignoring the whole tradition of the church.

This process leads to very good discussion about both personal and parish life.

"If the Church Were a Car..."

Have a picture of a car, or a toy car for a visual aid. Ask the group to imagine the church as a car. Then ask, leaving time to write down answers between each question: What part of the car is the Holy Spirit?....What part is the bishop?...What part am I (the leader, an active Catholic)?...Finally, what part are you?

Sharing the answers tells us so much about the participants' understanding of church, laity, hierarchy, God, and themselves. Everybody can answer these questions, though some may be more technical than others. These are some favorite answers: The Holy Spirit is—the model of the car, that special something that makes it what it is; the road map that shows us where to go; the air in the tires that makes the ride smooth.

The bishop is—the oil filter to keep out anything harmful for the church; the rear view mirror that keeps us aware of our past; the brakes! The active parishioner is—the antenna, keeping the church in tune with the world; the doors, inviting people in; the heater, keeping the church warm and inviting.

The inactive Catholic often identifies with a spare tire, or a passenger or even a hitchhiker. Obviously part of the program for returning Catholics is to help each person feel much more an essential part of the car.

A Paper Cup Parish

Form circle groups of about five people each. Each group gets a paper cup. That cup represents your parish (or the church, if you wish). It is to be passed in silence from person to person; each one is to do something to the cup before passing it on. Some people will put in doors or windows; some will decorate the cup; some may smash it, others gently caress it. When everyone is done, the members of the group explain to one another what they did and why, and the group can respond with their feelings about what was done. Those cups ought to stay around as a decoration through the rest of the sessions.

Teaching techniques like these are good only when they serve the purpose of the group. A good catechist does not fit the message to the technique, but makes sure that the technique communicates the message. Group leaders should always be on the lookout for creative adult education methods.

A Special Word About Scripture

It comes as news to many adult Catholics—active and inactive—that scripture is to be central in our personal and communal spiritual lives. An essential part of our catechetical ministry is to make that news sound like good news.

Copies of a good English translation (preferably the New American Bible or the New Revised Standard Version because they are used in liturgy) should be available for all participants. Most will need assistance in finding their way around in the Bible. Show them the break between Old and New Testaments, and the table of contents for each. Show them how to find the references for the coming Sunday's readings, and encourage them to read at least the gospel ahead of time. Use the psalms as prayer during sessions, and invite participants to read together directly from the scripture. When using a parable or other scripture story, help them find it and read along from their own copy.

Catholics need to be convinced that they know more of scripture than they think they do. Help the group verbalize and organize its memory of the stories of scripture. "What do you remember from the Bible?" "Do you remember any stories?" Years ago we learned Bible history rather than reading the Bible, but Catholics generally do know Abraham, Isaac, Jacob, Joseph, Moses, and David. With some prompting, they can recall the prophets and judges and some of the signs of God's saving power from the Hebrew scriptures.

Many of the parables and teachings of Jesus and the writings of St. Paul are familiar to Catholic ears because of their use at mass. *Every* time we have ever gathered for mass we have heard some of those stories. We do know them. We just don't know where to find them or how to quote them with confidence. Catholic neophytes in scripture study should look at Matthew 4:4, 6, 7, 10; Mark 11:17. In these and other places, Jesus quotes scripture just as many Catholics do today—"Scripture has it...." or "In the scripture it says..."—without specific reference to which book in scripture. We can know the message of scripture without the ability for specific references.

Once a person can begin to feel comfortable with scripture, a whole new world opens. In programs for returning Catholics, this comfort level should be a primary goal.

Teams can teach this message through both words and action. Probably minimal time will actually be spent in specific teaching about scripture. But the non-verbal teaching that can be most effective can pervade the entire process.

A copy of scripture should be displayed in a place of honor in the room used for meetings. That copy should be used regularly, for prayer and teaching, and the respect with which it is handled will teach volumes. It should be a goal of the session leader to make connections each week with the Sunday scriptures for that week—another non-verbal teaching that it is God's word that feeds and unifies our community action all week long. The stories of the people of scripture should become examples for issues being discussed. Take advantage of the rich resource of the people of our faith traditions. David sinned. Peter was impetuous. Sarah laughed at God. Elizabeth was infertile. Jeremiah was a kid. Joseph was treated unfairly by his brothers. Moses was unable to speak in public. Mary said yes without understanding everything the angel said. Introduce returning Catholics to some of their forgotten relatives, whose stories can inspire their own faith journey.

Honoring scripture, and opening returning Catholics to God's word spoken in it, is perhaps the greatest gift we offer the returning Catholic. "Indeed, God's word is living and effective, sharper than any two-edged sword. It penetrates and divides soul and spirit, joints and marrow; it judges the thoughts and reflections of the heart." (Hebrews 4:12)

"For just as from the heavens the rain and snow come down and do not return there till they have watered the earth, making it fertile and fruitful...so shall my word be that goes forth from my mouth; it shall not return to me void, but shall do my will, achieving the end for which I sent it." (Isaiah 55:10-11)

The word and will of God are powerful indeed!

Chapter 5

PRAYER, SPIRITUALITY AND THE RETURNING CATHOLIC

What Is Prayer?

Prayer is lifting our minds and hearts to God. Prayer is talking to God. Prayer is morning and night prayers, the rosary, novenas, vigil lights. Prayer is living simply through the day. Prayer is action on behalf of the poor.

Prayer is a word packed with powerful memories, feelings and expectations for both returning Catholics and the parish team meeting with them. The notion of prayer is necessarily tied to one's notion of God, and one's basic acceptance of oneself.

Addressing this constitutive element of faith life sensitively and honestly is key to ministry with returning Catholics. To pass over it lightly or simply as a class topic is to limit God's entree into the lives of the participants. To be insensitive to an individual's fears, preconceived notions and past experiences can have a damaging effect on a fragile faith life.

As in any group of adult believers, there will be among returning Catholics a great range of experience in prayer and in development of prayer life. One's prayer and spirituality is not tied to participation in a church community. Some people who have been inactive for a long time may still have a close relationship with God and a developed prayer life. Others may have so identified God and church that the experience of separation from church meant separation from God. Still others may have simply never considered the possibility of experiencing God personally. A woman expressed this so clearly at an initial meeting of Another Look: "What I want is to feel God's presence. I've tried many churches and it seems as though everybody else feels it, but I don't. I want that feeling."

Remember also that what people really learn and make their own in this area stays with them regardless of what their eventual decision may be regarding their return to active church membership.

Prayer is truly a lifeline for one who would be in union with God. The goal of any formation activity should be a feeling of comfort in the realm of prayer.

Prayer, Prayers, Pray-er

It is good to begin with helping persons to focus on where they currently find themselves in the experience of prayer. Look at the words PRAYER (describing an action or manner of expressing the self in communication with God), PRAYERS (those formulas which have helped people pray for generations), and PRAY-ER (the one who is praying). The goal, especially in ministry with returning Catholics, should be a sense of becoming and offering the "pray-er"—the self—to the God we have come to know.

The good news in that message is that each person's prayer is supposed to be unique. No one must follow another's method. Each person can "do it right" without meeting others' standards. For too long, many people have struggled to pray by putting their own specialness aside. They have ignored personal gifts, challenges, distractions, to fit their prayer to another's mold. Ministers need to find ways to help people be freed to be themselves in prayer. We don't have to get ourselves in shape before coming to God. We don't have to have it all together before we can pray. How welcome is the encounter that allows us to be only ourselves, fully ourselves, gloriously in need of our God!

Scripture presents ample images of those who became pray-ers, offering prayers to God in simplicity: David, who danced for joy before the ark; Moses, who addressed God in frustration over this stiff-necked people; Jonah who just *knew* God was going to relent and forgive; Peter who put *on* his clothes and jumped in the water, presenting himself with "Lord, I am a sinful man," St. Theresa of the Little Flower who was a pray-er because of only "little things," Catherine of Siena, a pray-er who argued and challenged communities and hierarchies.

Growing in Prayer

This is not the end of the spirit of prayer, however. While we do not strive to measure prayer by another's measure, we should move beyond our current experience and ability of prayer. Prayer is like the expansiveness of the universe. Where we are can be wonderful, very comfortable, and just challenging enough. But there are still new worlds of possibility out there where we can grow and become so much more than we already are. Each person can grow in prayer. There is always more, always a new word, a new image, a deeper insight that can change our prayer.

Perhaps this is the message that is newest for the returning Catholic. We are not now, nor will we ever be finished with learning prayer. It is not a matter of finding what feels good, nor of learning the right way, nor even of setting up good habits in which we persevere. Prayer is presence, as changeable and unpredictable as life itself. No matter how much we may wish it so, we are not what we were yesterday; no matter how hard it may be to believe, we will be different tomorrow. Our prayer must be all that it can be today. But we need courage to try what will be available for us tomorrow.

Teaching About Prayer

The courage to try something new in prayer is a gift that can come with the community of returning Catholics. In that group, after a few initial weeks, there can develop the safety to test out some new forms of prayer.

The first few weeks, that safety is probably not there yet. The group prayer needs to be simple and non-threatening, such as simply closing with Lord's Prayer recited together, with the traditional Catholic ending. Holding hands, adding spontaneous prayer or other prayer forms could prove uncomfortable for the first few weeks.

Early in the curriculum though, time should be spent on the topic of prayer. That experience prepares the group for more intentional prayer in future weeks.

Prayer Wheel

There is a discussion tool called a "Prayer Wheel." [See Figure 5.] After a short introduction affirming differences in prayer, each person takes time to fill in answers to the questions on the prayer wheel. They are shared first in small groups of about four each, and then with the larger group.

The questions obviously have no right or wrong answers, but they do allow a person to begin to talk about his or her personal prayer life. The responses of the group open up new vistas for most people.

"Where do you pray best?" Some people have never thought of praying in a car, or in bed, or in the shower. It is also a chance to encourage them to find a special place in their home for prayer. A place that is comfortable, quiet, and prepared for prayer will do some of the work for them in getting themselves ready to pray.

"What time of day do you pray most often?" affirms a basic flow of morning and evening prayer, but also can begin discussion of the image of praying always—the non-verbal prayer for solace or safety or patience or strength. Remind participants of the special significance of meal time prayer and night time prayer. They are the times we are most vulnerable as humans: when we are hungry, a sign of our neediness; and when we are about to sleep, a sign of our handing over our lives with peaceful trust.

"Do you prefer to pray alone or with others?" allows an easy affirmation that differences are okay. It also allows the team to speak of a needed balance between the two. One who prays only alone misses God's gift of community. One who has no personal prayer life comes to the community impoverished.

"One way my body gets involved in prayer is..." usually is the hardest question for people. Many people just say, "It doesn't." What a surprise when they are reminded of folding hands, the sign of the cross, kneeling, standing, the rosary beads, even fasting. This is a place where some of the richness of the Catholic faith tradition can be highlighted. It was taken for granted for so long.

A woman shares how the sign of simple open hands means so

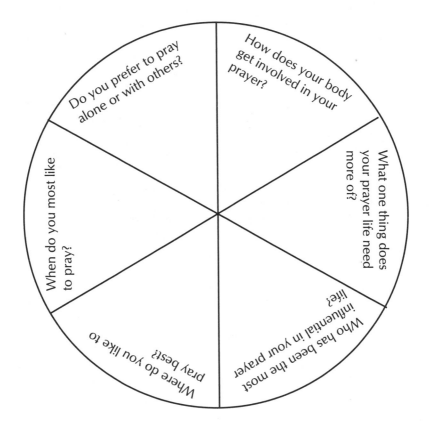

Figure 5. **Prayer Wheel.**

much to her. Whenever she feels the need for help, or the desire to pray, she simply opens her hands. Often she is unable to pray in words (during a class, for instance, or when in the midst of a counseling session with someone); yet with her body, she is able to pray.

This discussion leads to a renewed appreciation of the sign of the cross as well, in which we sign our bodies with the sign of our salvation.

"One thing my prayer life needs more of is..." usually leads everyone to talk about time. It is almost universal, among people who care about prayer, that they feel they want to pray more, which usually translates into more time. Suggest some of these words, which may not initially occur to someone: Energy (Is there a way to burn up calories in prayer? What kinds of energy do we possess?) Faith (What do you believe about prayer? Are all prayers answered? Does prayer always "work"?) Creativity (How might art, music, dance enhance prayer life? Could journaling help you listen to God?)

"The person who had the most influence on my prayer life is...." has been helpful in three ways. It usually deals with significant role models, and indicates what these adults feel they ought to be doing now. Most people talk of learning to pray from their mothers or grandmothers. Their attitude toward those early experiences probably color their current ability with prayer. For others, a more recent person has been most influential—a spouse, a good friend, even their own child. In such cases, the influence is usually more focused on their current conversion journey. Finally, this topic allows us to raise the question, "What influence does God have on your prayer?" How might God affect the manner and experience of your prayer? What would it mean for you to allow God to have that much power in your life?

Teaching about prayer may be the topic for just one week. The best way to learn prayer is by doing, and throughout your time together concentrate on *doing* prayer, and, when appropriate, talking about it afterward.

Prayer in Sessions

The class time spent on prayer has, as one of its primary goals, a level of comfort in testing out new forms of prayer. From then on, plan a variety of experiences that challenge participants to different kinds of prayer styles.

Centering Prayer

In centering prayer, a person is called to find within himself or herself a place for prayer. It involves a quieting of the body, mind and spirit to allow for a relaxed presence to our God. A leader or director is needed as one begins in this prayer. That person slowly gives the following directions:

"Begin by sitting as comfortably as you can in your chairs. Don't have anything in your hands or on your lap. Sit up straight with your feet flat on the floor and your hands open in your lap. Close your eyes, and begin to breathe deeply. Allow your breath to reach throughout your body, and then breathe out as completely as is comfortable for you. As you continue to breathe slowly and deeply, feel yourself breathing in all that is of God, all that is good and holy in your surroundings, and allow yourself to breathe out anything that would block God's entry to your spirit. Sit very quietly now; be as relaxed as you can be, and concentrate on your breathing. Allow God to fill your very self, as your breath courses through your body."

For beginners, about 3-5 minutes is enough quiet time at first. Call them back gently: "When you feel ready, open your eyes, and we will regather our attention as a group." Most people enjoy the physical relaxation that comes with this centering—our lives allow so little time for such intentional quieting. It will take some practice and experience for most to be able to put into words where God was for them in such an activity. It is, however, an excellent preparation for growth in prayer. Participants can come to learn that this can be done without a leader to prepare for any time in personal prayer, and is especially good as an entree into meditation.

Breath Prayer

When one becomes practiced in centering, the person can be challenged to find a *breath prayer*. A breath prayer is a short phrase, or simply a word, that one speaks easily with a breath. Sometimes it may be simply the name "Jesus," or another name that has special meaning in a personal relationship with God. It can be a short prayer — "Praise

you, Lord, in all creation" or "Have mercy on me, Lord Jesus Christ."
Whatever the word or phase, it should become sufficiently natural to
come without thinking, and should fit easily to the pattern of our
breathing.

Guided Meditation with Scripture

Guided meditation helps a person enter into a scripture story or
an event in the life of Jesus more fully. It can also be used to help a
person prepare for personal meditation. Often it is helpful to begin
with a familiar scripture story to call people into this kind of meditation. Consider using this kind of prayer to end the session on reconciliation. An appropriate gospel story to use is John 8:1-20, the story of
the woman caught in adultery. Prepare for such a meditative prayer by
beginning with a short time in centering. This is how the meditation
would develop:

"Listen closely as I read through this story. We have probably all
heard it before, but listen as if it were brand new tonight." (Read the
story through slowly.) "Now, I am going to read the story again. This
time, I want you to place yourself in the story as one of the characters.
You can be in the crowd. You can be one of the accusers. You can be
the woman. Or you can be Jesus. Prepare yourself to really be present
for this story. Imagine the sounds that surround you. There are many
people, and it is fairly noisy. Look at the sights that surround you. You
are in a crowded old city. See all the people who are there with you.
Imagine the smells of the crowds and the city. Feel the warmth of the
sun in this outdoor gathering space. Listen now to the action of this
story one more time, with you right there." (Read the story again, very
slowly.) "Allow yourself to stay in this story for a short time now.
Remember how you feel, and what is happening for you in this story."

People need a few minutes of silence after this, to allow their
feelings to focus. Then invite them back to attention with the group.
There should be time after such a prayer to share the feelings that
come. This sharing is best done in small groups, because the feelings
can be intense for the participant. What was really happening in that
story? How did you feel? Does this have anything to do with the experience of reconciliation?

The gospels are filled with stories that invite us to be right there on the scene. Consider using the coming Sunday's gospel in that way, or another story that would be significant in the topic for discussion for the evening.

Other Meditation Exercises

Guided meditation can also invite a person to meditation without the use of a pre-planned story. Participants can be invited to make their own story — to find God present in their meditation in a more immediate manner. For this, instead of putting yourself into an already written story, the person is called to make his or her own story.

"In your mind now, put yourself in a place where you are very comfortable. It may be a familiar place where you have been many times, or it may be just a place for your imagination, but it must be a place where you can feel comfortable. What does it look like there? Notice, with your mind's eye, the sights you can see. (Pause) What are the sounds that you hear where you are? Listen to those sounds. (Pause) What does it feel like there? Is it hot? Is there a breeze blowing? Do you feel sunshine? What are the feelings you feel in this place? (Pause) What are the fragrances you can smell? (Pause) Now, as you sit in this very comfortable place, invite Jesus to come to be with you. Allow Jesus to come to sit there right next to you. (Pause) Tell Jesus now what you would like to say to him. Talk with Jesus there next to you. (Pause) Now, listen to what Jesus wants to say to you. Listen to Jesus now. (Pause) When you are ready, allow your mind to bring you back to this place and this group." (Pause)

It is important to allow people time to share their feelings after a prayer like this. Some things may be too personal to share, so there should be freedom to speak or not as desired. This is usually very good for some people, and not helpful for others. It is a good opportunity to remind everyone that such differences are okay. Prayer styles should fit personal styles.

Spontaneous Prayer

The invitation to spontaneous prayer can begin as soon as the group has some feeling of comfort with one another. So long as a person feels okay to be quiet if he or she prefers to be quiet, it is fine to invite those who wish to speak to do so. Inviting prayers of petition at the end of the evening is a practice that can begin early in the process. Anyone who has a petition for prayer of the group is invited to offer it before the end of the evening. Set a clear pattern for that prayer, so that it is very easy for someone to participate. Team members model such prayers, by asking prayer for family, friends, world events, etc. "Lord, please take care of my neighbor who has cancer, and her three children." The group responds: "Lord, hear our prayer."

In future weeks, it is possible to expand the notion of spontaneous prayer, and also to move beyond prayers of petition. For instance, after a session on the history of the church, invite prayers of gratitude for people, practices or events that have blessed us in the church.

Sometimes, by the end of the process for a group, they are easily speaking prayers aloud, with little prompting. Other times, spontaneous prayer does not become comfortable for the group as a whole. Remember, the goal is to open up various vistas for prayer, not to insist on any particular one.

Formal Prayers of the Church

The prayers we learned as children have a privileged position in the tradition of our church. They have, for the most part, become part of our prayer treasury as a church because they have been helpful over centuries and across cultural barriers. Those prayer traditions should be honored. Participants in programs for returning Catholics always appreciate getting a copy of those prayers which allows the individual the chance to decide how to make them part of their life now. "Catholic Prayers For Everyday" is a small handout available from the Paulist National Catholic Evangelization Association. They cost only five cents each, so they can be made available broadly.

Two prayers—the Lord's Prayer and the Creed—hold a position in our community that is unique. Their position is acknowledged most clearly in Christian initiation. As catechumens near the Easter vigil and their full initiation into the community, the church gives them its two prayer treasures. The rites are called "Presentation of the Lord's Prayer" (#178-183, RCIA) and "Presentation of the Creed" (#157-162, RCIA). In entrusting catechumens with the Lord's Prayer, the community acknowledges the relationship with our God that we share, a relationship that allows us to call God "Abba," Father—loving, gentle Parent. That prayer carries with it relationship with Jesus, and with one another. It also expresses the way of life of a Christian. To present it to a catechumen, or to invite a returning Catholic to claim it anew, is to provide the opportunity for that person to acknowledge acceptance of that way of life. Truly praying that prayer has ramifications far beyond saying the words themselves.

The Creed is our statement of faith. To entrust it to a new member, or to share it again with a returning member, implies a full acceptance of that person. Those who can pray the Creed together speak their faith, the words that hold what is deepest in the heart. "I believe" comes from the old English word that means "I have set my heart on." It is speaking what is deeply held within. Whether you use the Apostles' Creed or the Nicene Creed, the experience of praying the Creed together should be one of reclaiming all that is desired by the heart of the church.

These two prayers also are regularly part of our celebration of eucharist. That means that the experience of using those prayers in other settings can be regularly brought back to consciousness when they are used at mass. Focusing on those prayers becomes part of total preparation for participation in liturgy.

Morning prayer and evening prayer from the Liturgy of the Hours are other formal prayers of the church that are often a surprise to returning Catholics. As more parish communities gather to celebrate these prayers together, they become more available to individuals. There may also be someone in the group who would be interested in learning to pray the Liturgy of the Hours privately, aware of being united with the church in that prayer.

Music

Saint Augustine said, "The one who sings, prays twice." Music allows us to express feelings, and to pray as a community in an especially gifted way. Depending on the talents of your team and the participants, music can play a significant role in sessions for returning Catholics.

If musical talent is minimal in your group, find tapes that can be used for reflection, and consider that one of the most important lessons to be learned might be that even without a great voice, singing in church can add to the worship experience. Singing with a tape can work. Even better is singing as group with the best leader of song on your team. Someone will at least be able to get the group started.

If you are lucky enough to have a musician on your team, take full advantage by including music every week in prayer times or at breaks.

Returning Catholics should learn the "new stand-bys" (as opposed to the *old* stand-bys). "Here I Am, Lord," "On Eagles' Wings," "Be Not Afraid" and "The Heavens are Telling" are all songs that have meaning for returning Catholics, and are sing-able enough to be remembered by participants. In addition to these, ask your music minister to make tapes of some of the hymns being currently used in the mass at the parish, so that participants can be familiar with them ahead of time. Try to schedule one meeting where the music minister spends some time with the group to teach them the setting for the acclamations at mass (Holy, Holy, Mystery of our Faith, Great Amen and Lamb of God).

Music attracts some people more than others, but the ability to pray in song with others seems to be a significant step on the journey to *feeling* Catholic again. One who will not—or perhaps cannot—be free enough to sing has burdens that still need to be lifted. Music is essential.

Prayer with Spiritual Masters

Moving back to full membership with the church involves building and rebuilding relationships on all kinds of levels. One of those levels can involve getting to know a new friend or companion on our spiritual journey. The great spiritual masters who are part of our Catholic tradition are becoming much more accessible to laity than ever before. Introducing returning Catholics to such people and their prayer styles can have dramatic effects on that person's spirituality.

Paulist Press has a series of the works of spiritual masters (*Classics of Western Spirituality*) that make them available to ordinary people. The parish should have or at least know about such literature, and the team can make recommendations as indicated to individuals. What surprises are in store for one who comes to understand the classic method of prayer of St. Benedict (listening, waiting, experiencing), or one who meets for the first time the freshness of Julian of Norwich, whose feminine and earthy images give a new language for prayer, or one who comes to a new appreciation of the absolute trust in God lived by Francis of Assisi and expressed in his rule of life.

Developing Spirituality

Prayer is but one visible aspect of a person's spirituality. It does not contain one's spirituality, but rather expresses it. Spirituality is more all-encompassing of life. It is our pervasive way of viewing life that affects everything else. While the term may be new to returning Catholics, it should not be a wholly unfamiliar concept.

Our world today speaks a language of spirituality. It offers its own suggestions for what is to be worshiped, what is to be the goal of spirituality. One such kind of "spirituality" holds the body as all-important. Exercise, fitness, and vitamins can become like "prayers" offered out of such a "spirituality." "Taking care of Number #1" is another "spirituality" offered around us. Success, security, material things become the measure by which we evaluate our lives. These are real spiritualities in our world. They capture our spirits, change our values, suggest an ultimate goal for life that is sure to disappoint. Yet they are so tempting.

It is the language of spirituality that challenges the person at the deepest level. The attention paid to prayer finds its primary meaning in the developing spirituality of the participant. Spirituality is like being in love; praying is like doing acts of love. Spirituality is like an expansive bay that lies open before us; praying is like finding a channel, an inlet, protected waters on the bay. Spirituality is like the ocean; praying is like the wave we ride, or the one that washes over us. Spirituality is like having competence in a particular field; praying is like doing a job well on a given occasion.

The spirituality we offer is so simple. It is first of all a Christian spirituality: Jesus is central. God first loves us. God is revealed as Trinity. Secondly, we are offered a Catholic spirituality: we are centered on the eucharistic table. We find God present and active in the sacraments.

This is the goal of our attention to prayer with returning

Catholics—not to end with good practices, but rather to help them find what God has placed within them. What is it that leads to true happiness, to fulfillment? What is the meaning of life? For whom are we created?

Chapter 6

RITUAL NEEDS OF
RETURNING CATHOLICS

Speaking the Language

Ritual action and the language of symbol allow human beings to communicate on the deepest level of reality. It is the most human form of communication. Only men and women are able to make symbols, and to enter into ritual activity. It is part of the human experience to long to be understood—to express those feelings, thoughts, realities, that go beyond what words can contain. We make symbols, we do rituals, and their power becomes much more than the purely physical reality could hold.

An American flag, for instance, is a symbol. It becomes for all Americans an important sign, one that evokes emotions and memories. It becomes a motivation to action for some. But as with all symbols, there is not precision or clarity in specifically what it evokes. It is powerful as a symbol, but its effect varies greatly.

Thanksgiving dinner is an American ritual. Clearly, that night's dinner is more than a normal meal. Each family has its "rules" for Thanksgiving, its menus, its traditions. Accepting them and participating in them—or rejecting them and saying no—takes on much more meaning than a slice of turkey has in itself.

The realities of our faith lives are even more dependent on symbol and ritual for expression. Belief, reconciliation, community, eternal life—all are concepts beyond expression with words. They need the language of ritual.

The sacramental and liturgical life of the Catholic Church is filled with such language. Water, light, oil, bread, wine, touch, allow us who understand to experience, communicate and know more deeply. The role of ritual in faith life is crucial. It affirms what we are experiencing, connects it to the experience of the community, puts us in touch with others who understand, and allows us to gloriously express the inexpressible.

The Ritual of the Mass

The primary ritual for us as Catholic Christians is the mass —the "source and summit" of our life in community, according to the Constitution on the Sacred Liturgy of Vatican II. Celebrating the eucharistic liturgy both makes us who we are as church, and allows us to be what we are supposed to be in the world. The "obligation to attend Sunday mass" is real, because it is that community, the worshiping assembly, which really is the church. That action renews each week our faith in Jesus' life, death and resurrection, and our commitment to one another as a believing people. We are in communion with one another in symbol and ritual as we participate in eucharist.

That communion is experienced as well in ministry and in stewardship. People who have the same faith can work as comrades as they live out their lives. What do you do with your time? How do you expend your energy? How do you spend your money? The communion of liturgy becomes the source for communion of ministry and stewardship.

One who is out of communion, who cannot feel or express the faith that is within, yearns for reconciliation, for the symbol ritual that brings about the forgiveness, the peace, the union that it signifies. Returning Catholics need to ritualize, they need to express in symbol what is happening to them. The return to participation in that language of mystery is like coming home for a Catholic who has been unable to communicate for so long.

The Sacrament of Reconciliation for Returning Catholics

Clearly, the eventual celebration of reconciliation is a significant part of the journey of a returning Catholic. That will signify the welcome back to the eucharistic communion of the church, as well as a return to the ministerial communion to which each member is called. That experience should not be taken lightly by either the participants or the church community. Preparation for it on both sides allows it to be the personal, truly reconciling event it is meant to be.

We have much to learn about reconciliation from its history, and from our current understanding and practice of the sacrament. More so than most parts of church life, this sacrament is different from what our personal past experiences might have suggested.

The Beginnings of the Sacrament: Penance

The earliest roots of this sacrament are found in the clear experience of Jesus' absolute intent to forgive sin. There was no question about whether or not sinners who came to Jesus would be forgiven. Jesus always welcomed them, and forgave the sin. In the early church, such forgiveness came a little harder for a community that was so tightly knit. They could welcome into their number those who *had been* sinners. Baptism washed all that away, and began the new life for the Christian. But for someone who sinned *after* baptism, it was another question.

Remember that entrance into the community came after long periods of preparation, and that the community needed to trust one another deeply because of the opposition to Christianity from outside the community. Remember also that sin in those days meant very serious public actions, which clearly cast doubt on the whole community, not just the sinner. (Murder, adultery and apostasy—denying the faith in public—were the kinds of sin in question.) It was very hard for the community to forgive such actions. The fact that there was at least some path to reconciliation available shows the presence of the Spirit in the church, calling it throughout its history to continue to do what Jesus had done—to forgive.

The sacrament of penance in those days was hard to receive, and was not available easily. By about the third century, it had taken on a form that included the penitent's being enrolled in an Order of Penitents, in preparation to receive sacramental reconciliation in the church. That time of preparation was extensive, and involved doing some public practice of penance to make known to the whole community the sincere desire to repent. The penitent would be welcomed back by the bishop, usually in preparation for the celebration of Easter. This process intentionally paralleled the journey to the sacraments of initiation, and was seen as a kind of second baptism—a second chance at this new life. But there would not be a third chance. Penance was available only once in a person's life.

While this experience is quite distant from our experience of the sacrament today or anytime in our lifetime, it does contain in it some key parts of the meaning of the action of the sacrament:

1. It emphasizes that forgiveness is essential to the nature of the church. There is no question that the church must have a way to forgive, to offer reconciliation, if the church is to be true to the example of Jesus.

2. The community has to be involved in the forgiving. Our practice of this sacrament is not simply about God's forgiveness. A real community is affected by the actions of its members. It is not enough for the community to be a channel of God's forgiveness; it must be able to forgive as a community as well, and to express that forgiveness in practice and in spirit.

3. One who participates in this sacrament is expressing real repentance. This is not an empty ritual, but one that is filled with meaning, with newness. On the part of the penitent, there is an expression of a real change that is intended.

The Sacrament Changes: Confession

A major change came in the experience of this sacrament around the year 900. People began meeting individually with monks. They would confess the failings and weaknesses of daily life, and receive forgiveness from the monk. This form of the sacrament came about because of the recognition of people's desire to be better than they were. Ordinary people, living ordinary lives, were not involved in those serious public kinds of sins that called for the public and structured experience of the rite of penance. But they did recognize that they were not living the full life that they had been called to in Jesus. People were ready for a kind of spiritual direction, some help in personal spiritual growth. They saw the need for God's help in overcoming the weaknesses and faults they found in their lives.

These early experiences seemed very far removed from the sacrament of penance. There was no bishop. It was a less formal event, with only a penitent and a monk or priest present. The sins that were discussed were personal sins, failings in one's individual walk with the Lord. But it soon became apparent from the experience of the people that this was a more helpful and needed channel of God's forgiveness and the grace to live out one's baptismal call. Very soon, this form of the sacrament became the most common, and then the only way to receive the sacrament. The common name for the sacrament became "confession," as the emphasis was placed on what was said by the penitent. The practice found its way into the structures of the church in the confessionals that became part of church buildings, and into the training for men who would be priests for their role of confessor.

This form of the sacrament is the one in which most of us were trained. While there have been changes since Vatican II in our practice of the sacrament, some of the elements of this form of the sacrament remain with us as signs of how we are meant to experience reconciliation with God and our community:

1. Our relationship with God and the church is lived out in our very personal, very ordinary lives. The choices we make, the way we live out our relationships, our responsibilities—these are the proof of our baptismal life.

2. A confession of sins—our statement to another human being of our failings and faults—focuses our desire to improve. A commitment to "be better Christians," or a general profession of sorrow for sin, can be too generic. To say "This is what I have to do differently," "This is where evil is present in my life," is to take a first step in making the changes that will make a difference.

3. Christian life is an ongoing journey of conversion. We need spiritual guidance and personal contact along the way.

After Vatican II: Reconciliation

Vatican II called for a revision of each of our sacraments. It was necessary to look at what the symbol and ritual were to communicate, and then to evaluate how effective that communication was. If changes were needed to make the ritual and symbol more alive for our church today, they were to be made. Penance was the one of the first sacraments considered, and the result of that study is the revised rites of reconciliation that guide our practice of the sacrament today.

In many circles, the more common name for the sacrament has

become "reconciliation." That name aptly describes the more fundamental change in emphasis for the sacrament. No longer do we emphasize the *penance,* what one does to prove the integrity of the repentance (though there still is a penance). No longer is our *confession,* the words we say, the most important part of the sacrament (though there still is a confession). Rather, the focus is on the *reconciliation,* the effect of the sacrament. We are one again, able to be in communion. We are welcomed home again.

The revised rites reclaim the communal nature of this sacrament by recommending communal celebrations for reconciliation, while maintaining the value of individual confession of sins.

Our church is not finished yet—not even for our day—with the developing nature of the sacrament of reconciliation. We must always be open to how God's Spirit is moving us to express in our own day the forgiveness of our God, and the reconciliation we seek with our community of faith.

Awareness of Sin

From the beginning of the formal experience of sacramental forgiveness in our church, the practice of the sacrament has paralleled the experience of sin for the people. When sin was understood as major public actions, the sacrament was formal and public. When sin was understood more commonly to be personal minor imperfections, the sacrament became personal and frequent.

The rites of reconciliation available to us today offer a range of experiences of forgiveness that help us deal with our experiences of sin today. We are also finding other avenues for healing and reconciliation within the church, which may or may not be connected to the traditional experience of the sacrament.

Experience of sin today seems more complex than it did in the past. There are at least three ways people talk about sin today; each calls for a different kind of ministry from the church.

A Need for Forgiveness

The first is the experience of having done something that we know is wrong. We feel guilty, we regret our action, and we need to be

forgiven. This is the experience of sin most of us had as we were growing up, but it is still a real experience today. It is the one most easily
dealt with in the experience of individual reconciliation. There is the
opportunity for us to acknowledge what we have done, to express our
sorrow, and to hear and feel the forgiveness of God and our church
community.

A Need for Healing

The second experience of sin is more that of a weakness or dis-
ease afflicting our spirit. It is not so much an individual action,
although actions do indicate its presence; it is more pervasive; it might
be expressed more in the terms of the awareness that what is ought not
to be. An example of this kind of sin can be found in relationships
among family or friends. We can become aware of a growing distance,
a refusal to communicate, a readiness to blame the other. We know this
is not what the relationship should be, but we feel something growing
between us that just is not right. It may seem to be no one's "fault."

This experience of sin calls for an experience of healing more so
than forgiveness. In the sacrament of reconciliation, one is able to
describe the feeling of weakness, the situation that exists which is
beyond our ability to overcome. God's grace in such an encounter is
better described as healing than as forgiving. The effect of the sacrament is experienced in the healthier relationship that exists when the
power of evil has been overcome.

Healing services are a somewhat new phenomenon in the
Catholic Church. Twenty-five years ago, such events took place only
in charismatic communities, and were more focused on expected physical healings. Today, in some places, healing services focus equally on
the need for spiritual healing, and people who are burdened with this
kind of experience of sin may be served well by the prayers of the
community in this way. The sacrament of reconciliation can be made
available for individuals as part of, or after, such a time of prayer for
healing.

A Need for Deliverance

The third experience of sin is one more related to our modern
society. It is the experience of an evil that holds us in bondage, an evil

over which we have no control. It is expressed in words like these: "I just can't help it, but..." Perhaps this is something young people deal with especially as they battle the power of peer pressure. The allure of what the world names as good can so overwhelm us that we feel powerless. When one recognizes such an evil in one's life, what is needed is an experience of being set free, an experience of salvation, of having the bonds broken.

People are often more able to experience this kind of grace when the communal rite of reconciliation is celebrated. With the presence of the whole community, one is able to face the evil that surrounds us, that holds us trapped, the evil to which we contribute by silence or by acquiescence. Together we call on our God for salvation, and we are able, as a community, to move on in freedom.

Because of the richness present in the sacramental action of reconciliation, it is helpful for a person to know what he or she needs from the sacrament. Expanding the possibilities for naming how sin is present and affects our lives also expands our expectations as to how God can forgive, heal, save us from that evil.

Celebrating the Sacrament

It is most natural that a group that has come together for the purpose of considering returning to full membership in the church should have the opportunity to celebrate the sacrament of reconciliation together sometime before the formal time together ends. As you plan for that celebration, keep the following principles in mind:

People must be free to participate at various levels. (Not everyone will choose to have individual reconciliation, for instance.)

It must express the joy of true reconciliation.

Each member of the community must feel support.

It needs to be relaxed.

It needs to be enough like what they will experience in the sacrament afterward that they can recognize it.

It needs to be personal, so that it is true symbol of expression for the real people who are involved.

Here are some examples of reconciliation services that could have meaning for a small group that has been together for several weeks:

The Good Shepherd

The service happens in church.

Materials needed for the service: slips of paper and pencils; a suitable container for a small charcoal fire for incense.

Theme: The Good Shepherd

Opening hymn: "The Lord Is My Shepherd" (on tape)

Theme setting discussion: What does the image of a good shepherd mean to you? The readings this evening talk of a slavery that is ended; a returning sheep carried gently on the shepherd's back; there is no recrimination about having been away.

1st Reading: Isaiah 40:1-5, 9-11 ("Comfort my people....Like a shepherd, he feeds his flock").

Gospel: Matthew 18:12-14 (The straying sheep is found with great joy).

Shared Homily: How can we allow God to be a good shepherd for us?

What are the demands on our lives when we choose to follow the shepherd?

Do you believe the good news of forgiveness?

Have you been carried back to the community?

What does reconciliation feel like for you?

Guided examination of conscience:

(Give out pencils and small slips of paper. Instruct the participants to jot down their answers to these questions on separate sheets of paper.)

What has to happen in your life for you to experience reconciliation?

Have you been hurt? Do you need to forgive?

Who are the people you need to forgive?

For what hurts does the church need your forgiveness?

Are you ready to forgive?

For what do you need forgiveness?

What needs to change about your life for real reconciliation to happen?

Which of these are you ready to let go of? For which are you ready to forgive or be forgiven?

Those pieces of paper can be placed in the container that has burning coals. They will begin the flames that will burn the incense. (If there are slips of paper one is not ready to deal with yet, they can be kept in one's wallet or pocket — someplace they will be seen frequently. Each time, ask God to give the help needed to be able to let go of what is blocking reconciliation.)

At this point, those who will receive reconciliation are invited to do so.

At the end of the service, the incense is brought out, and all the participants are invited to stand in a circle to be incensed, recognizing the holy people they are. The group then joins hands to close with the Lord's Prayer and a sign of peace. The evening ends with refreshments and a celebration.

Some Other Options

The theme for the closing service should be chosen based on what the experience of the group has been. The image of the seed and the sower can be meaningful. 2 Corinthians 9:6-10 tells us: "God loves a cheerful giver....He will multiply the seed you have sown...." John 12:24-26 tells the story of the grain of wheat falling to the ground and dying, in order to bear fruit.

As you prepare any ritual service, be sure to consult the readings of the day in the church. They often have just the right message for a liturgical gathering.

The symbols used should be simple and clear. They should not have to be explained. They should be a channel of communication, not the focus of it. The first example used incense. Other appropriate symbols include ashes, candles, water, the cross.

Other Reconciling Rituals

Sometimes reconciliation is not an appropriate way to conclude the experience of a program for returning Catholics. This may be because most people have already received sacramental reconciliation; or because of a number of participants who are not yet free to do so, either because of personal hesitation or because of a legal impediment. Here is a sample of an alternate closing ritual that includes a renewal of baptismal promises:

Theme: We need the support of community on our journey

This service is held in the room used for meetings each week. It should be set up in a way that sets a prayerful tone. In a prominent space should be the paschal candle and a bowl of water with a sprig of greenery in it. Quiet music playing in the background helps to focus the group to prepare for prayer.

A team member welcomes the participants and describes why the room has been set up the way it is.

Greeting and call to prayer

1st Reading: 1 Corinthians 12:12-26 (the analogy of the body; we need one another).

Gospel: John 15:9-17 ("Love one another....You are my friends....It was I who chose you").

Homily: Invite sharing from participants around the readings and the feelings they engender.

Opportunity To Renew Baptismal Promises

Explain the significance of getting back in touch with our baptism.

Everyone is invited to stand to respond to the questions asked by the celebrant.

Do you reject Satan? (We do) And all his evil works?...

Do you believe in God the Father Almighty, Creator...

This is our faith...

The renewal of baptismal promises can be found in the Rite of Christian Initiation of Adults or in any other text for the baptismal ritual.

Each person is invited to approach the bowl of water, and make the sign of the cross in silence, and then return to be seated. After appropriate time for this, all stand and join hands to pray the Lord's Prayer together. The sign of peace leads to an informal closing. The prayer should be followed by a closing celebration with refreshments and music.

Other, less formal prayer closings could be focused on a particular scripture reading. The prodigal son certainly lends itself to such an experience. An extended time for Imaging Prayer (as described in Chapter 5 of this text) around that story, especially if it also included time for journaling and then sharing with a few others, could be an appropriate concluding ritual for returning Catholics.

What About Public Rites?

Some people who minister to returning Catholics see the value of celebrating public rites during the journey with those who are experiencing the deep conversion involved in moving from alienation to a full return to the community. The model would be parallel to the experience of Christian initiation. It presumes an extensive outreach preceding the season of Lent that would invite those who would be ready to celebrate Ash Wednesday as an enrollment into the Order of Penitents. Those people would then enter the season of Lent as their time of final preparation for reconciliation. The community benefits from the sign of their repentance by acknowledging its own need for repentance and change through the season of Lent.

Such a journey comes to its culmination on Holy Thursday, when the penitents are welcomed back to the eucharistic table through a ritual called "Return to the Table of Witnesses and Prophets." The penitents come in with the entrance procession, reverence the altar, and remain in the sanctuary during the liturgy. They are the first to approach the table to receive eucharist that night.

These two public rites parallel their experience of the sacrament of reconciliation. Sometime near Ash Wednesday, they meet individually with a confessor and tell the story of their journey (confession), and on Holy Thursday they meet again with him to receive absolution to prepare for the celebration of the triduum. The experience of these rites is part of the Re-membering Church Workshops available through the North American Forum on the Catechumenate. A parish team should consider the possibility of such public rites, as well as looking for other ways to allow the community to be aware of and to benefit from what is happening to returning Catholics.

Other Ways to Involve the Community

If you do not choose to celebrate those formal rites, the community can still be included at least through announcements, prayers of the faithful and bulletin articles. For instance, on a regular basis—not weekly, but about once a month—mention those in the community who are part of a journey back to full membership. It can be done before mass, in words like these: "Members of our parish program for returning Catholics are with us this morning. Please pray for them especially as they continue on their journey back to full membership in our community. Remember also our responsibility to be examples to them, and to everyone around us, of our own commitment to our God and to one another."

Or it can happen in a more generic manner, like this: "For those who are considering returning to active membership in our community, let us pray to the Lord. . ."

The goal of the public nature of these actions is twofold: (1) to keep the community aware of those returning to full membership, and (2) to surround the returning member with the prayer and love of the whole church.

The Spirit of Reconciliation

The rituals and symbols that express and bring about reconciliation must characterize the whole experience of any program that serves returning Catholics. It begins with the very first meeting. Hospitality, coffee, chairs in a circle, smiles, handshakes, laughter all carry the seed of reconciliation. They say, "You are accepted here."

The opportunity to tell one's real story provides the ground for the seed of reconciliation to grow. Whatever your story is, you are still accepted here. Parish staff people, particularly the priests who serve the parish, have a unique and indispensable role in reconciliation. They will be the channel for sacramental reconciliation; their friendly presence during breaks, or at the beginning or end of sessions, opens that channel. Participants need to view the confessor as a friend.

Our sacraments are celebrations of what is going on in our lives. Nowhere is that clearer than in the case of a returning Catholic who comes to readiness for reconciliation. It is the real celebration of God's forgiveness, the church's forgiveness, and often, also, the forgiveness of the church by the returning Catholic. We are one again and at peace, ready to continue our journey in the company of our community of faith.

Chapter 7

WHAT ABOUT THE REST OF THE PARISH?

When a parish community is seriously open to returning Catholics, the rest of parish life cannot remain unaffected. It is not business as usual. The spirit, the skills, the motivation behind reaching out to the inactive affects the rest of the parish as well.

An Evangelizing Community

Chapter 2 detailed a major one of those parish-wide effects—the development of an evangelizing spirit among all parishioners. One who is challenged, empowered, encouraged, enabled to evangelize will never be the same again. Such a person experiences the power of the Spirit working through him or her in the life of someone else. God's grace has been visible, tangible. The evangelizer always receives as much as the person evangelized. Because ministry to the inactive requires such participation of average parishioners, it touches the parish at large in a very personal and effective way.

Such ministry also requires real openness and a welcoming spirit on the part of parish leaders and staff. One does not turn such a spirit on and off depending on which person you are addressing. Personal concern and a caring spirit, an openness to listen and a non-judgmental attitude become habits. The definition of parish ministry includes the word "evangelizing."

There are several other more specific areas where parish ministry will be challenged: helping people needing annulments, family concerns for children who have not had religious formation, and a need for ongoing community to support the recently returned Catholic.

Helping with Annulments

Accurate information is perhaps the greatest need in the area of annulments. People outside the church generally have false notions of what annulments are about. Unfortunately, too many Catholics, and even some parish leaders, share those misconceptions and that misinformation. Even people who have been through an annulment can make the mistake of generalizing from their own experiences.

Yet parish ministry, and especially ministry to returning Catholics, will often call for dealing with a need to become involved in the annulment process. The parish team must understand the basics of the process, and know how to help people who are involved in it.

Our attitude toward the annulment process is important. There are two underlying factors that can help us appreciate the reasons behind the process. First, a marriage is a holy relationship, very much a part of how we live out our lives in the Lord. Scripture uses the image of married love as a sign of God's love for us, a love that is life-giving, faithful, and dependable. True married love—whether the partners are Catholic or not—is a sign (a sacrament) of God's love for the world. The church believes in marriage as something holy and worth protecting. Every marriage is presumed to be a valid marriage. This is why the church "gets involved" in marriages of people who are not Catholic. We presume God's presence in any marriage relationship.

Second, people who find themselves in a marriage that is not what it should be are in need of pastoral care and understanding from the church. The annulment process can help people understand what has happened to them, and put it behind them. The process is designed to be a pastoral outreach to people in need. It is truly unfortunate that there are so many stories that relate bad memories of annulments. Often they are second or third hand, or they are stories told by those who chose to give up at the first look at forms needing to be filled out. Be assured that there are good stories out there too.

A woman has shared her experience: "Finally," she said, "somebody cared about what had really happened. The divorce was all so impersonal. Nobody cared to hear how I had really tried to save the marriage. Nobody cared to hear what our feelings were. The annulment process helped me understand what had really happened to us. They cared about me, and helped me feel better about myself."

Another couple described their experiences in the process. They both needed an annulment in order to marry in the church. They applied, but with an attitude that they characterized as "show me." Was the process really based on making money? They asked for a payment plan in which they would pay ten dollars a month; they filled in the forms and sat back to "wait and see." What they discovered was help from the tribunal staff, not hounding for payment. This couple uses their experience to try to convince others of the real purpose of the annulment process— to help those in the community who have this special need.

Getting the Facts

Here are some facts about annulments that can be helpful:

1. Annulments in the church are not the same as legal annulments. Legal annulments declare that there was no marriage; an annulment in the church declares that the marriage was not a *sacramental* marriage, although it may have appeared to be so.

2. The status of children of a marriage that receives a church annulment is not affected in any way. They do *not* become illegitimate.

3. There are extensive forms to be completed at the beginning of the process. The questions call for telling the story surrounding the beginning of the marriage relationship. The story is often from long ago, or one that has been suppressed in memory; but it is the place where it all began, including, in most cases, what went wrong in later years.

These forms look for, among other things, the real ability to make the free mature decision to marry that is required for sacramental marriage. Did the partners understand and intend the permanent commitment of marriage? Were they mature enough in chronological and psychological age to make such a commitment? Were there outside influences limiting the ability of the partners to make the decision freely? Filling in these initial forms is usually the hardest part of the whole process. Once they are completed, the rest is fairly simple by comparison.

4. There is a need for "witnesses" to give some corroborating information. These are other people who knew the couple around the time of the marriage. They are asked to complete a fairly simple form that asks questions about the couple at the time of marriage. (If such witnesses are not available, other possibilities exist.)

5. The annulment process involves the legal system of the church. The tribunal is the church court. There are advocates and defenders of the bond (church lawyers), and an automatic appeals system that includes another diocesan tribunal system. There is testimony and evidence, and decrees are issued. While the language remains cluttered with "legalese," the person applying for an annulment does not personally experience any kind of courtroom drama.

Their role is almost exclusively completed as paperwork in the privacy of one's home, on one's own schedule. There is an assignment of a skilled advocate who helps as much as requested. That person will meet with someone personally, and assist with the forms if requested; or the entire process can usually happen through the mail or on the phone.

6. There is a cost for the process that varies by diocese. The charge is partial support of the expense to the diocese of the tribunal system. No one is to be denied access to an annulment because of an inability to pay the fee. (A simple annulment in the archdiocese of Baltimore, for instance, costs about $350. If there are special circumstances that require additional people or time for the process, the cost would increase. Expense in your diocese may be higher or lower.)

7. Sometimes for a marriage in which at least one party is Catholic, there can be reason to grant what is called a "decree of nullity" based on "lack of form," which is not the same thing as an annulment, but has the same effect. This happens when the rules of the Catholic Church were not followed completely in the ceremony of marriage. (Remember, these rules apply only to Catholics.) In such a case, regardless of what else happened, the first marriage is declared not sacramental. This process is much simpler, faster, and therefore less expensive than the annulment process.

These few paragraphs about annulments certainly are not enough to make someone an expert on the annulment process. Hopefully, they do give enough basic facts to dispel some myths about annulments and perhaps enough of a taste of the process to allow you to be helpful to others.

What Else You Can Do

There are several ways local parish ministers can assist others in the process:

You can help convince someone that each situation is unique. What happened to your friend's cousin — or anyone else — does not determine what will happen to someone else.

You can help the person be in touch with those who can give the necessary assistance; you can help to make sure that those people follow through with the one needing help.

You can give encouragement and prayer support to the person throughout the process.

The priests in your parish are the first line of support in applying for an annulment. They will either be able to help directly, or they will know diocesan policy about getting into the annulment process. Permanent deacons are also often very helpful in this kind of work.

Finally, people in your parish who have been through an annulment process themselves can be a rich resource. They need some preparation — they must remember not to make promises, and not to generalize from their experience — but they can give valuable witness and helpful companioning throughout the process.

Family Concerns

I remember a story told by the great catechetical leader, Christiane Brusselmans: A mother once came to a preparation meeting about first communion. At the end of the session, she said, "Excuse me, Sister, but there is one problem — my child has not yet been baptized." "No problem," said Sister. "We can help you with that." The mother was so pleased, she decided to continue. "I have an older child too. He is in the fifth grade, and has never been baptized." Sister said, "No problem. We can help you with that." "There's a teenager too," said the mother. "He's been baptized, but nothing else. Can you help him too?" "No problem!"

The mother was trusting now. "I'm ashamed to say it, Sister, but

I have never made my first communion. Is there hope for me?" "No
problem," said the Sister, ready to introduce this mother to the parish
Christian initiation team. "One more thing, Sister. The man that I am
living with; I don't think he has made his first communion either."
..."*Now*, we have a problem."

Stories like this are not at all uncommon when ministering with
inactive Catholics and their families. The final twist of the story raises
one set of questions about sexual lifestyles in today's world; the point
of the story for this chapter, however is the rest of the story—about
family members and their varying levels of relationship with the community. Church documents have long reminded us that sacraments are
not connected to an age or grade, but there is still the cultural
Catholicism of second grade first communion and "finishing up" with
confirmation at some later grade.

These practices are deeply imbedded in the minds of most inactive Catholics who may feel most guilty at being "late" with sacraments for their children. It is so important that the parish leaders who
work with them do not feed those feelings. We have to be able to say
"No problem!" with meaning.

Parish experience today, especially in evangelizing parishes,
calls for really being ready for those exceptions to what may be the
more common practice. Children beyond seven or so who have had little or no faith experience need some special help. In most cases, the
structure and format will follow guidelines for children's catechumenate. The official document for the Rite of Christian Initiation of
Adults, Part II, #1 is entitled, "Christian Initiation of Children of
Catechetical Age."

It gives some general guidelines for helping such children experience a personal desire for sacraments as a sign of a genuine developing faith life. For children already baptized, whether in the Catholic
community, or in another Christian church, there need to be appropriate adaptions made, just as we make adaptions for adults involved in
Christian initiation. The principles of children's catechumenate call us
to focus on a child who has little or no previous faith experience. If
that is the situation, whether or not that child is baptized, the proper
journey for the child is one based on the children's catechumenate.

Parish experience with children's catechumenate usually
involves separate groups of children meeting apart from the regular

religious education time. Consider scheduling those sessions at the same time as meetings for returning Catholics and those in the Christian initiation process. Children are usually grouped according to age and grade. The range depends on the children involved in a given year. A group may successfully gather a variety of ages with a skilled catechist who is able to have older students helping younger ones. Or there may be a group for lower grades, and another for older children. These groups use catechetical materials that present the broad overview of our faith, for the dual purposes of allowing the child to feel comfortable in knowing what the faith life of this community is really about, and preparing the child to enter the regular religious education program in the coming year. Several publishers are now making such materials available to assist in children's catechumenate work. (See the resource section of this book for some references.)

Additionally, the children should celebrate the major rites of Christian initiation as arranged for children, and be dismissed each Sunday to a sharing around the liturgy of the word (separate from the adults, of course).

Catechists who work with these children see real personal involvement and growth on the part of their students. Indeed, they do come to feel an ownership for their profession of faith and celebration of the sacraments. It is not possible for them to slide through because their parents want it. Complementing the conversion centered formation program at the parish is the powerful effect of a family where God and church are newly found and appreciated. Indeed—when we are ready for them—there is certainly *no problem!*

Teenagers

Helping teenagers in such circumstances provides different challenges. Some older teens are best served meeting with adults. They have a definite good effect on the dynamics of an adult group. Sometimes teens are best served with a periodic special group that builds on the ongoing youth ministry experiences in the parish. Sometimes teens need an ongoing group just for them. Teens less often come just because their family is experiencing something. They may wait a year or so to move toward church themselves. On the other hand, sometimes it is the teenager who calls the rest of the family to a community that helps one find meaning.

Parish ministry to inactive Catholics is not simply an adult ministry. Returning Catholics have children who will need to be accepted as readily and fully as their parents are accepted. Look at all the variables involved in helping the children: How old are they? Are there any learning problems? What sacraments have they received? What is their level of faith experience? You can't have all the plans ready before you start. As people gather and needs are made known, the parish leadership is challenged to find way to meet those needs. We must be able to say with assurance, "No problem."

Community Experience

Possibly the most significant results of conversion centered ministry in a parish—Christian initiation and outreach to returning Catholics—is the growing awareness that adult believers need community. We have experienced the truth that the Spirit works in community; that human beings need community; that change and growth happens most naturally within the safe environment of a community; that personal relationships—not just with a pastor or a teacher, but with one another—are the key to that elusive feeling of belonging that sustains us through the hard times.

One Parish's Story

For over ten years, St. Joseph's parish has been involved in ministry to the inactive as well as consciously working toward the development of small Christian communities. That work began formally seven years ago by inviting the parish into a Lenten experience of small group discussion. They used two programs: *To Follow His Way* (available from St. Anthony Messenger Press) and *Spirituality of Parenting* (available from Sheed & Ward). About three hundred people signed up for those six week programs. They met in one another's homes and, with the help of a member facilitator, discussed scripture and its connection to their daily lives. It was a new experience for almost everyone, and positive enough that it helped the parish council decide to call for full parish involvement in doing RENEW in the parish, for the purpose of starting permanent small Christian communities. (RENEW is a long-term program of small group faith sharing, published by Paulist Press.)

RENEW helped over the next two and a half years to build and maintain small groups, and the process of faith sharing. RENEW provided a framework on which to build toward the ultimate goal of ongoing small Christian communities. By the second season of RENEW, some inactive Catholics were being affected. RENEW groups could be a safe first step if a person was at all considering looking at the church again. RENEW groups became a "feeder" for Another Look.

When RENEW ended, the parish had been involved in building permanent small Christian communities for three years. The parish now calls itself a community of communities, and there is a commitment to sharing faith and building relationships whenever they come together as parishioners. Ten percent of adult parishioners are part of a small Christian community, and the number is growing. It is clear that the sense of belonging to church, of having ownership for church, of being the church and being welcomed by the church, now happens on a variety of levels.

A small Christian community *is* the church—a community gathered by faith, around God's word, sharing lives and prayer with one another. It is connected to the larger church in the parish and the diocese and the universal church; but there is growing awareness that in one's small Christian community, it is truly *church* that is being experienced.

This phenomenon has been a tremendous help in ministry to returning Catholics. Still, there is the dynamic of small Christian communities sending inactive Catholics to Another Look. But there are now two other dynamics going on. A person who has returned to full membership is not simply sent out into the church at large. Most now are rather called into a small Christian community, where their conversion journey continues with support and challenge. In a community of nurture, where each member gives and receives, the recently returned Catholic continues to grow by receiving and by having the opportunity to give to others. The communities are also challenged, from inside and outside, to more than self-nurture. Faith felt and shared quite naturally becomes faith in action in the world.

The other phenomenon is that some returning Catholics do not need a specific group for returning Catholics at all anymore. Small

Christian communities can be the primary locus for the formation needs the person has. Such companioning may not be possible in every small Christian community, but there may be some who have the special gift for welcoming and reconciling inactive Catholics.

Resources for small Christian communities are included in the final section of this book.

The Whole Church

Local parishes become renewed and invigorated as they evangelize and truly welcome in and welcome home those who were once outside the community. What about the rest of the church?

It is always important to help people realize that the local community is not the whole church. A returning Catholic who has needed a healing process because of past hurts in the church may be hurt again. We are not a perfect community. Other parishes, diocesan regulations, interpretation of church documents, a tired staff person—all can be cause for undoing the good work that has been begun, unless people have been prepared for our real church. There are many warts and blemishes, but it is still the closest we can come to the church Jesus founded for us.

We are a community of saints and sinners. Mother Teresa is our sister as truly as the parish staff member who hurt our feelings; the Catholic scandal on the front page of the paper happened in the same community that feeds one thousand homeless people every day. Being ready to be family with that whole church is good preparation for the rest of our lives. There will be rocky times. It is better to know how to ride out the waves than to expect to be able to avoid all of them.

The presence of saints and sinners in our church can be good news too. Experiencing conversion is wonderful, truly a high point, a gift, a grace from God. We are changed, and life is different afterward. But we do not stay on that mountain top. Sometimes we fall, sometimes we get overwhelmed by the ordinary, sometimes we are more sinner than saint. How important it is to know that the church does not leave us! We are family—usually, all of us doing our part and traveling in the right direction. But when one of us falls, or gets tired, or scared—the others are there to help. The Spirit is truly present in the church Jesus gave us. We are never alone.

Chapter 8

GETTING STARTED

So, what next? How do you help your parish get started in ministry to returning Catholics?

Forming a Team

Once you feel drawn to this ministry, it is important for you to test out that call by talking with several other people. Share your vision, your perception of the situation in your parish, and your own willingness to work toward this goal. You need a combination of parishioners and staff members; whichever you are, you must begin by gathering others who are also caught by the vision you present.

Look for parishioners who have themselves been inactive for a time and have returned to full membership in the community. (In an average group of Catholics adults today, about one-half have been inactive for a period of two years or more.) Expand your horizons to find partners different from yourself. A team benefits from variety in age, marital status, profession, personality style. Find at least two or three others who share with you a desire to offer themselves as channels for the compassion of our Lord to the inactive Catholics in your community.

Involve your pastor, and the other priests of your parish. Their position gives them a unique window on the soul of your community. Their wisdom and experience are essential as you work to plan your course of action. Their ministry as confessor and reconciler will ritualize the culmination of the work you do. Their role is crucial. This does not mean that they must be directly involved in all the aspects of this ministry. It is quite appropriate that laity form the leadership team. Laity can do the planning, the outreach, the listening, the teaching, and much of the reconciling. The pastor, however, is the link with the rest of the church; the pastor has the official voice of the whole community. This ministry of reconciliation cannot be done without him.

Parish councils or other leadership bodies are an important ally. Presenting the needs of inactive Catholics in your community to such groups can win you valuable support. It is a fair guess that many members of such councils have some loved one who is inactive. The hope of some help for those we know and love is very good news.

Parish Goals and Objectives

What would happen if the parish council chose to make reconciliation a parish-wide goal? One parish did, in these words: "This parish is, and is perceived as, a reconciling community—that is, we understand and use the sacrament of reconciliation; we help people experience reconciliation in their families, small groups, and in the parish community at large; and we are a welcoming and accepting community." After three years, there was not reconciliation with everyone, but they did learn what it means to be working toward reconciliation, to listen to those with opposing views, and to spend the time needed to wait for reconciliation.

It was that goal that inspired open meetings where council, staff and others listened to parishioners who disagreed with some direction of the parish. Much time was spent trying to discern where the Spirit was leading the community, amidst differing views that were so strongly held. Educational outreach increased dramatically, as multiple channels were employed to explain what was to be done.

The parish council gave strong moral support for all effort toward reconciliation, including the specific outreach to inactive Catholics.

The Staff

The rest of the staff are also important allies in beginning this ministry. They usually have broad contacts throughout the parish, to assist in identifying those in need, as well as recognizing others suited to ministering in this kind of outreach.

Once you have found others with whom to begin, and once you have the affirmation of the pastoral leadership of your parish, BEGIN! One is never prepared for everything that might happen. It may seem that God always finds a way to keep us just a bit off balance. These reminders help us remember that in this, as in our lives and in all true ministry, it is God who is in charge. Our job is to do what we can, to use the gifts we have been given, to stay open to the gifts our co-workers bring, but, most of all, to simply let our spirits stay open to God's Spirit.

If we are to be good ministers, especially in evangelizing work, we must be something like something like a kite being flown. Sometimes we fly high and beautiful, and people say: "Look at that wonderful kite." Sometimes we struggle with short bursts and twists and turns, and sometimes we fall flat on our face. In the work of evangelization, God flies our kite, on the wind of the Spirit. We really do not need to worry about how we are doing. But we do need to be there, and to release ourselves to the kite flyer's skill.

The Underlying Attitude

An effective minister to inactive Catholics is characterized by two outstanding features: love for each person we encounter, and love for the church.

To Love Each Person

What does it mean to love each person we encounter? It means we respect them; we believe what they say; we see them as the free responsible persons they are; we have a stance of unconditional positive regard for them.

Such an attitude is the opposite of approaching others with pre-conceived judgment. Sometimes, when we hear the story of why someone left the church, it is hard not to feel "That wasn't all that bad," or "She should have spoken up and said how that made her feel." The listener must be able to hear, accept and believe the story being told. It is a story of what happened to this individual person. What we hear is the effect it had on him or her, which is more than may have actually happened, and is usually more than what was intended to happen. If a person *felt* it, the effect is there, and that is where we must begin.

We hear misinformation; we hear anger and frustration; we hear longings of a human heart shut off from a community of faith. Our response must be to help the person discover the way out of the situation. The process works when adults are able to discover a new way to see the past and envision the future; it works when adults feel safe enough to reveal their real hurts and accept the healing ministry of a supportive community; it works when adults know they are free to choose a return to the church or a move in some other direction, without fear of condemnation.

It usually does not help to tell people what they ought to do; it is not helpful to use judging language like "right and wrong," "good and bad"; anything that implies that a person must move in a certain way limits that person's ability to experience the inviting grace of our God. We meet God when we do so willingly. What we encounter when we are forced, whether by positive or negative powers, is less than God.

Our job is that of a helper. Help is defined by the helpee, not the helper. We are not there to defend the faith. We are not there to save people from sin. We are not even there to show people what is best for them. We are there to be a channel of God's grace, God's invitation, God's love and compassion. The best tools we have are our own good spirit, our own inviting actions, and our own love and compassion.

To Love the Church

What does it mean to love the church? It has to do with feeling at home, feeling a spirit of family, feeling as though you have been through a lot together. The image of family carries much meaning when applied to our relationships as church. We really have little to say about belonging to a family. We are either born into a family or chosen by the family in adoption, claimed from outside to belong here. So it is with our church. Even those who join as adults often feel that it is because of something outside drawing them to "cast their lot" as it were with this community, these people. We are claimed in baptism and confirmation not only by our God, but by the community that feeds us eucharist. We are chosen, called, born into a church family in which we hope to be nurtured, challenged, and taught to be free. We are put in relationship with one another by virtue of our relationship with God.

As with a family there are good times and bad. Some family members have a harder time than others, and sometimes there is favoritism. One always remains a member of the family, even if the individual walks away and changes his or her name. Family reminds us who we are and where we have come from, even when—perhaps especially when—we would rather forget. And family is (supposed to be) where you can always depend on finding understanding and support. Family is (supposed to be) where you can always come back. Loving the church means being family in the church.

Loving the church also means accepting the church as it is. This does not mean that we should not try to change things that should be changed, but it does mean that we look at the church as it *really* is, and not as we might want to pretend it to be. This is the same dynamic that is present in a love relationship. Do we love an ideal that we have for the person, or do we accept and love the person as he or she is, and then encourage the best from that person. One who loves unconditionally can be much more effective in calling the other to change than one whose love is conditional on the change. Such limited love is not focused on the other, but on our own image of what we want the other to be for us.

Loving the church means calling it to be all that it can be. It means caring enough to work to see that the church is faithful to its call to be Jesus present in the world today. Not giving up, but rather working unceasingly and accepting the challenge with love are signs of true and loyal love for the church.

Loving the church is not blind obedience. It is not holding fast to a set of teachings or practices from the past. It does not mean defending the church against any and all detractors. Witness statements about our own experiences of church, of help and support in times of need, and our feelings of belonging, are far more powerful than standing up in a defensive manner to refute someone else's negative statement or experience. The church is a community of disciples, not of orators and lawyers.

Such a balanced attitude of love for the person and love for the church puts the minister in the position of real service. There is no need to defend, to force, to convince or to save. One is simply called to be the bridge, the connecting link to allow easy travel between the two.

One who enters this work with only one of these two loves will have a hard time being the effective connecting link. If you love the church, but do not really accept the person, it will be very difficult to communicate with them effectively. If you love the person, but have problems with love for the church, you may be more therapist than minister in group gatherings.

How About Those Who Feel They Cannot Return?

There are some situations in which people feel they just cannot be reconciled with the church. In some cases the person still genuinely loves the church, but simply experiences such a draw to something else that that "something" must be followed.

Many women find themselves in such a situation. They describe a strong, clear call to ministry that is not open to them in the Catholic Church at this point. For them, in most cases, it is with great sadness that they search out other Christian communities in which they can fulfill the call they feel. Other women with similar feelings remain with the church, and work to challenge and change structures that they experience as unjust.

Spanish-speaking people in the United States, in growing numbers, are leaving the church that seems to ignore their language and culture, and embracing small evangelistic communities that have spoken to them in their language and their lifestyle.

There are those who have left the Catholic Church to join the religious community of their spouse. The choice for family unity has often been thoughtfully made, and for many such people it is a permanent decision. They do not see themselves as having left the church, but as building a new life of faith with their new family.

In cases like these, with decisions made clearly and thoughtfully, the person does not see himself or herself as an inactive Catholic, and indeed feels very much a member of another community. Certainly, we should respect the decision made, and not imply that their faith choice did not matter. However, to respect someone else's decision does not simply mean saying "Goodbye and good luck."

A Prophetic Message?

There are two reactions that seem to be indicated when dealing with such a person who has left the community with what could be called a prophetic message. First, we must try to appreciate and hear the prophetic message in their action. Whether or not our decision would have been the same, our response should attempt to understand the feelings that caused the decision. What was there in the church that led this person to feel the need to leave and find another community? What was lacking in the Catholic Church that could have been there?

Prophetic action is usually hard to hear, but once we really hear it, it is not so hard to understand. It can be a very positive force for the church to learn the proper lessons from these cases.

The second reaction is to maintain some friendly relations with the person who has chosen to leave. It could be something like the invitation that is sent to a family reunion, even to relatives we have not seen or heard from. Even those who have rejected previous invitations are still welcome, and we let them know that through an occasional invitation to a special event.

The meeting with the local bishop described earlier in Chapter 2 is just such a special event that can attract some of these people who have made a decisive move away from the church. They come to tell their story, and, having told it, both they and the community are better off.

It is important to know about and respect these special cases among those who have left the church, but the vast majority are not currently active in another community. They are rather among the unchurched. Pope Paul VI named those inactive Catholics among the unchurched as the number one focus of our evangelizing ministry.

When the Inactive Catholic is a Member of Your Own Family

Almost every Catholic family today has at least one member who is not actively involved in the church at this time. Statistics tell us that a majority of all young people between the ages of fifteen and twenty-five leave the active practice of the faith for a period of at least two years. These statistics hold true regardless of the religious formation the young person has had, whether in Catholic schools or in parish religious education programs.

The other side of those statistics holds some better news. Most of those young people who leave (about sixty percent of them) do return to the church at some point. On this side, religious formation does make a difference. Those who had regular religious formation (in a Catholic school or a parish program) that was supported by family practice are the ones who return. Those whose formation was sporadic and separated from family practice are less likely to return.

It is hard to avoid the question: "Where did I go wrong?" We keep searching for an answer that can explain what happened. Most of the time, there is no satisfactory answer. The perfect family of faith has not been found! We all make mistakes, but also most of us did more good than harm. The same family system often produces both active and inactive Catholics.

What Is the Church Doing?

The reality of today's situation would suggest that it is not particularly helpful to be finding a place to put the blame. Religious educators and church leaders in general are struggling to make the parish part of a young person's formation more effective. Youth ministry guidelines call for a true holistic approach to supporting the faith life of young people. The field of catechetics is focusing on the evangelizing potential of their work, supporting personal growth choices and conversion experiences that are inspired by the message being shared. Children's liturgies of the word are an exciting step in the direction of a child's full participation in mass, and in connecting faith formation directly with community faith practice.

Family involvement is clearer and more frequent. Recognizing and highlighting the role of the family, a child's developing spirituality becomes an ongoing part of developing life, not a separate phenomenon. Sacramental preparation and celebrations have become key points for bringing children to own their Catholic identity. By separating sacraments from a class activity or a grade level, they call for purposeful participation by the child and the family.

What Families Can Do

All of this happens as the church struggles to respond to the situation of young people in the church today. It may have effects in the next generation of young Catholics, but for our loved ones who are now inactive, perhaps these points can be helpful:

1. Give them the same respect, freedom and unconditional positive regard given to those outside your family. We tend to be much more demanding on our family; we really believe we do know what is best for them. It is very hard not to "should" on them. Families do of course have the right and responsibility to insist on certain things as part of family life. That often includes regular mass attendance "as long as you are under my roof." But young people who have moved out, or who achieve some independence through becoming self-supporting, do have the right to make decisions about how they will live their lives. Sometimes, even before that point, a reasonable, loving and pastoral decision may be to allow a younger person to stay away from mass when participation really becomes counter-productive.

Whatever the circumstances, a young person deserves the love that allows the possibility for faith decisions that are different from our own.

2. Evangelization has to do with *invitation.* It is not coercive and not overbearing. What we say to our loved ones must be invitational. It should sound inviting. "Why would I want to do this if I have said I am not going to church anymore?" Special days or events, or family activities in the church, might be such an invitation. Christmas mass, a special program for young adults, a wedding or baptism — all can provide a reason for an invitation. Invitations also can be accepted or rejected without recrimination. If the answer is no, do not let it build up a wall.

3. The faith life of the family in your home remains a powerful drawing force. Prayers at meal times, religious symbols, the respect shown for the Bible, your personal prayer life, all speak volumes to those who share your home. Make the most of those signs.

4. Look for opportunities for spiritual discussions (as opposed to "church" discussions). Questions about the meaning of life, what really counts in the end, what a true friend is, why people die, provide an entree for discussing deeply spiritual issues. When a new baby is born into your family, or a young person falls in love, or cancer strikes someone you know, it calls for a spiritual understanding. Too often we stay on the edges of those real-meaning discussions, because to enter into them is to be surrounded by mystery. We are no longer in control of where we go next. Take the plunge into the mystery of God on those

occasions. Invite young people into those discussions with you. Our words may be clumsy. Indeed, we do not fully understand the mystery ourselves. But that is where God is. Finding the Holy there draws us closer, and helps us experience the need we have for our God.

5. Never underestimate the power of prayer. We do what we can do, give the best example we can, and then, persevere in prayer for our loved ones. Perhaps the prayer should not be, "Lord, bring my daughter back to the church," but rather, "Lord, I entrust my child to you. Help her know your love for her, and lead her in your path."

6. Finally, remember that somebody else may well be the one who can best reach your loved ones. People who gather as inactive or returning Catholics in parishes usually tell of their family upbringing, of learning to pray, and feeling the value placed on the church. Parents may never hear the compliments paid them! The journey back often needs the assistance of others in parishes. As you work to help others, there will be others out there who are in a position to help those you love.

CONCLUSION

The challenge of ministering to returning Catholics can appear to be an overwhelming one. The need is so great. It calls for sensitivity on so many levels. The range of gifts required is so large. It would be easy to say, "I really don't think I can handle this." Let me close with a story told so often by the late Father Alvin Illig, who was Director of the Paulist Catholic Evangelization Association. He really understood the challenge of evangelizing, yet he more than most people knew how important it was to unleash the evangelizing potential in the laity of the church.

Jesus had an interesting way of dealing with what we call limitations! In Chapter 6 of the gospel of John, we hear about a day when there were thousands of people following Jesus, listening to his preaching. In his usual manner, Jesus felt concern for the people as mealtime approached. He said to Philip, "Where shall we buy bread for these people to eat?" Philip began to list the problems. It was an impossible task!

In the midst of the crowd, there was a little boy—a child, who often can teach us so much about forgetting the problems. He had a lunch. We can just imagine his good Jewish mother preparing him for the day with a hearty brown bag meal of bread and fish and figs and cookies. She would never have let him follow the crowd without something to eat. Well, he heard the discussion going on between Jesus and the apostles. It was probably hard for him to get Mr. Philip's attention—after all, he was only a child. But, finally, he did, and he offered what he had.

93

Philip must have felt a little silly even mentioning it to Jesus. After all, what would this little bit mean when the need was so great? But, Philip didn't have a better idea, so he went to Jesus: "There is a lad here who has five barley loaves and a couple of dried fish, but what good is that for so many?" (Do you notice that there was only bread and fish left? He was, after all, just a little boy. Along the road he had already eaten the cookies first, and then the figs, so all that was left was the bread and the fish, or else the story would have been called the multiplication of the loaves and the fish and the cookies and the figs.)

"What good is that for so many?" But then, Jesus accepted the boy's gift. "Jesus took the loaves of bread, gave thanks, and passed them around to those reclining there; he did the same with the dried fish, as much as they wanted." Not only had the little boy's gift been enough to go around, but they needed twelve baskets to collect the leftovers!

The totally insignificant gift that had been given by the totally inadequate giver became enough, when it was given to Jesus.

Whenever we feel inadequate to the task, whenever it seems that our gifts will be insignificant in the face of the need that exists—remember what happens when our gifts are offered to Jesus. The work, after all, is the mission of Jesus. Our ministry of evangelization, and in a special way our ministry to help returning Catholics, is ministry placed in Jesus' hands. Our gifts *will* be insignificant, by themselves; we *are* inadequate to the task, by ourselves. But in Jesus' hands, it becomes enough.

RESOURCES

About Inactive Catholics

George Gallup, "Attitudes of Unchurched Americans Toward the Roman Catholic Church," The Gallup Organization, Inc., 53 Bank Street, Princeton, NJ 08542, 1985.

Dean Hoge, *Converts, Dropouts and Returnees,* The Pilgrim Press, 132 W. 31 Street, New York, NY 10001, 1981.

"Another Look," Paulist National Catholic Evangelization Association, 3031 Fourth Street, N.E., Washington, D.C. 20017.

Helpful Books for Returning Catholics

Becoming Catholic, Even If You Happen to Already Be One, J. Killagon, et al., ACTA Foundation, Chicago, IL, 1980. (The title is perfect, the book not quite so. Someone using it individually would benefit from the reflection aids and focus questions. A group would probably use it more like a teacher's manual, and possibly another book with more informational content would also be requested by participants.)

Catholicism Today: A Survey of Catholic Belief and Practice, Matthew Kohmescher, Paulist Press, 997 Macarthur Blvd., Mahwah, NJ 07430, 1989. (This book presents what we believe as Catholics in understandable language for today's church. The way that it builds on traditional language is especially good for people who have been away from the church. For instance, in the chapter on "Healing and Reconciliation," after discussing terms like satisfaction, confession, reconciliation and sin, it deals with questions like, "Is confession worth it?" and "When should a child's first confession take place?" The chapter on God deals with "The Existence of God," "The Gender of God," "God and Me," and "Who Is God?")

The Great Mysteries: An Essential Catechism, Andrew Greeley, The Seabury Press, 815 Second Ave., New York, NY 10017, 1976. (This is a good presentation of most of the major areas of questioning for returning Catholics. What is best about the book is its dealing with our faith as mystery, connecting faith and life issues with theological insights. Chapter headings deal with issues like: "The Mystery of the Cross and Resurrection"—Why is there evil in the world; "The Mystery of Holy Eucharist"—Is it possible to have friends?; "The Mystery of Heaven"—Why is life not fair?)

Books Designed for Use with Christian Initiation (can also be helpful as references for participants, according to their interest and educational level.)

Illustrated Catechism, Redemptorist Pastoral Publication, Liguori Publications, One Liguori Drive, Liguori, MO 63057, 1980.

The Teaching of Christ, Ronald Lawler, O.F.M. Cap., et al., *Our Sunday Visitor, Inc.,* 20 Noll Plaza, Huntington, IN 46750, 1976.

About Adult Education

Christian Religious Education, Thomas Groome, Harper and Row Publishers, Inc., 10 E. 53rd Street, N.Y., NY 10022, 1980.

Helpful Books for Children's Catechumenate

Benzinger Publishing Company, 15319 Chatsworth Street, P.O. Box 9509, Mission Hills, CA 91395. *Come To the Lord,* Sr. Blanche Twigg, M.H.S.H. (for intermediate grades, plus teacher's manual).

Redemptorist Pastoral Publications, Liguori Publications, One Liguori Drive, Liguori, MO 63057. *How You Live with Jesus* (for intermediate grades); *Jesus Loves You* (for primary grades).

William H. Sadlier, Inc., 11 Park Place, New York, NY 10007. *Our Catholic Faith*, John Barry (for intermediate grades).

About Initiation of Children

Robert Duggan and Maureen Kelly, The *Christian Initiation of Children,* Paulist Press, 997 Macarthur Blvd., Mahwah, NJ 07430, 1990.

About Small Christian Communities

Arthur Baranowski, *Creating Small Faith Communities* and *Pastoring the Pastors,* St. Anthony Messenger Press, 1615 Republic Street, Cincinnati, OH 45210, 1988.

Thomas A. Kleissler, et al., *Small Christian Communities: A Vision of Hope* and *Resources for Small Christian Communities: A Vision of Hope,* Paulist Press, 997 Macarthur Blvd., Mahwah, NJ 07430, 1991.

Bernard Lee and Michael Cowan, *Dangerous Memories, House Churches and Our American Story,* Sheed and Ward, 115 E. Armour Blvd., Box 419492, Kansas City, MO 66141, 1986.

About Annulments

Annulments: Your Chance to Remarry in the Catholic Church, Joseph P. Zwack, Harper and Row, 1700 Montgomery St., San Francisco, CA 94111.